BILLIONAIRE HABITS
FOR ENTREPRENEURS

DR. STEPHEN AKINTAYO

DISCLAIMER

This book is not intended for use as a source of legal, business, accounting or financial advice. All readers are advised to seek he services of competent professionals in legal, business, accounting and finance fields. While reasonable attempts have been made to ensure the accuracy of the information provided in this publication, the author does not assume any responsibility for errors, omissions or contrary interpretation of this information and any damages or costs incurred by that. While examples of past results may be used occasionally in this work, they are intended to be for purposes of example only. No representation is made or implied that the reader will do as well from using any of the techniques mentioned in this book.

The contents of this book are based solely on the personal experiences of the author. The author does not assume any responsibility or liability whatsoever for what you choose to do with this information. Use your own judgment. Any perceived slight of specific people or organizations, and any resemblance to characters living, dead or otherwise, real or fictitious, is purely unintentional. You are encouraged to print this book for easy reading. However, you use this information at your own risk.

IMPORTANT LEGAL INFORMATION

DEDICATION

To God almighty for the life-changing ideas and revelation in this book;

To my Father and mother, who were the first to open my eyes to business and real estate;

To my beautiful wife and mother of my children;

To every entrepreneur seeking godly financial breakthroughs in their businesses and personal life;

I dedicate this book to you all.

ACKNOWLEDGEMENTS

My utmost gratitude goes to God Almighty, the maker of men, for He has made me out of nothing.

Thanks to my family for their contributions and support, especially my lovely wife and understanding children.

I gratefully acknowledge the recognition and support of my spiritual and business mentors.

To all members of staff of Gtext Holdings for their feedback and unending support and encouragement, I appreciate you all.

I also appreciate my team at Stephen Akintayo Consulting for working tirelessly to put this work together.

I love you all!

CONTENTS

BILLIONAIRE POTENTIAL SELF-ASSESSMENT TEST

To what degree do the statements below correspond to you?

a: Totally Disagree, b: Somewhat disagree, c: Somewhat agree, d: Totally agree.

1.   I love to open myself up to new challenges when I take on a new project

Totally disagree (b) Somewhat disagree (c) Somewhat agree (d) Totally agree.

2.   I am fairly at ease in difficult situations

Totally disagree (b) Somewhat disagree (c) Somewhat agree (d) Totally agree.

3.   Where others see problems, I see possibilities

Totally disagree (b) Somewhat disagree (c) Somewhat agree (d) Totally agree.

4.   I always worry about what others may thing before embarking on an important step

Totally disagree (b) Somewhat disagree (c) Somewhat agree (d) Totally agree.

5.   I am fairly curious and I am continually in search of discovery

Totally disagree (b) Somewhat disagree (c) Somewhat agree (d) Totally agree.

6.   I am not less effective in stressful situations

Totally disagree (b) Somewhat disagree (c) Somewhat agree (d) Totally agree.

7.　　　　I want to build something that will be recognized publicly

Totally disagree (b) Somewhat disagree (c) Somewhat agree (d) Totally agree.

8.　　　　When faced with difficulties, I look for alternative solutions

Totally disagree (b) Somewhat disagree (c) Somewhat agree (d) Totally agree.

9.　　　　For me, what counts is action

Totally disagree (b) Somewhat disagree (c) Somewhat agree (d) Totally agree.

10.　　I am able to imagine how I and others can achieve results

Totally disagree (b) Somewhat disagree (c) Somewhat agree (d) Totally agree.

11.　　When I embark on a project, I am confident and positive that I will carry it out successfully

Totally disagree (b) Somewhat disagree (c) Somewhat agree (d) Totally agree.

12.　　I aim for excellence in everything that I do

Totally disagree (b) Somewhat disagree (c) Somewhat agree (d) Totally agree.

13.　　I believe that I can somehow make my own luck

Totally disagree (b) Somewhat disagree (c) Somewhat agree (d) Totally agree.

14.　　In general, I always trust my instincts

Totally disagree (b) Somewhat disagree (c) Somewhat agree (d) Totally agree.

15.　　I have challenges working for someone else

Totally disagree (b) Somewhat disagree (c) Somewhat agree (d) Totally agree.

16.   I try to be the best in the area of my competence

Totally disagree (b) Somewhat disagree (c) Somewhat agree (d) Totally agree.

17.   For me, risk taking is like a ticket, it is a question of chance

Totally disagree (b) Somewhat disagree (c) Somewhat agree (d) Totally agree.

18.   I am able to see solutions to problems

Totally disagree (b) Somewhat disagree (c) Somewhat agree (d) Totally agree.

19.   I always want to have the final say

Totally disagree (b) Somewhat disagree (c) Somewhat agree (d) Totally agree.

20.   I can easily foresee many ways to overcome a challenge

Totally disagree (b) Somewhat disagree (c) Somewhat agree (d) Totally agree.

21.   I can easily motivate others to work with me

Totally disagree (b) Somewhat disagree (c) Somewhat agree (d) Totally agree.

22.   I am resilient, I am able to pick myself back up after a fall or failure

Totally disagree (b) Somewhat disagree (c) Somewhat agree (d) Totally agree.

CHAPTER ONE
HOW TO IDENTIFY AN ENTREPRENEUR WITH BILLIONAIRE HABITS.

"Owning and running are different things. Billionaires own multiple businesses, but they only run one."

WHO IS A BILLIONAIRE?

Let's begin with definitions, shall we?

As stated, a billionaire is a person who has a net worth of $1 billion or more. In other words, if you can sell all of your assets for cash, pay off your debts, and have $1 billion remaining in the bank afterwards, you are a billionaire. On the other hand, having $1 billion in assets with debts of $900 million doesn't make you a billionaire. However, you and your family are unlikely to worry about future college expenses or retirement.

CHARACTERISTICS OF A BILLIONAIRE ENTREPRENEUR

i. They engage in mutually beneficial relationships

Years ago, my family and I lived in a suburban part of Lagos state, Nigeria. We lived an average, comfortable life by the day's standards. Eventually, God started blessing me, and I began to travel outside the country. Suddenly, people started paying attention to my family and me. It reached a point where the attention we were receiving in the community was unnecessary and starting to make us uncomfortable. I recall how on several occasions when I returned from a journey, the commercial motorcycle operators (popularly known as Okada men) in the community would sight me from a distance and quickly run to inform my wife that I had returned from my journey. It began to look like we were the ones in the entire community who travelled more often. As a result, I had to tell my wife that it was time to leave that neighbourhood. I told her, "We cannot continue to live in this neighborhood and look like we are the richest. That is not a good omen. We should move to a new place where we will be challenged." My idea was to move to a new place where what we had would be considered nothing by community members. That way, we would be challenged to do more and achieve more. And that was what happened. I remember how after moving to our new location, I woke up the following day and stood by the balcony of our storey building and, upon glancing at my neighbour's compound to the right and seeing the types of cars he had. I suddenly realized that the least of his vehicles was ten times better in value than my only good car. To be sure, I looked at my neighbour's vehicles to the left, and the story was the same. Then I thought, "Yes, we have made the right decision. We have moved to the right environment. Now we will hustle and work hard to climb up." And that was precisely what eventually happened. By moving to a new location, we were consciously challenged to work harder than before to meet the social expectations of our environment. As I write this, we are considering moving to a new location that will be more challenging than where we currently are. We may move to Banana Island in the next couple of months; who knows? I shared this personal anecdote to make the point that your environment, network of influence, and social circles are essential factors to consider when making wealth. The fact is that your network plays a significant role in your financial attainment which is one of the secrets of billionaires.

ii.   They think win-win

"If you must succeed in life, you must make sure that the people you allow into your circle are people who add value to you and you, in return, add value to them."

This scenario can be described, in the words of Stephen R. Covey, the author of one of the best books ever written on personal development, The 7 Habits of Highly Effective People, as a Win-Win relationship. According to Covey, the most effective interpersonal skill anyone can have is to think win-win. "Win-Win is a frame of mind and heart that constantly seeks mutual benefit in all human interactions," Covey wrote. He said, "Win-Win means that agreement or solutions are mutually beneficial, mutually satisfying. With a Win-Win solution, all parties feel good about the decision and feel committed to the action plan." One of the most profound things Covey says about this philosophy is that "Win-Win sees life as a cooperative, not a competitive arena." Because billionaires understand this principle, it is one of their major principles.

Unfortunately, many poor people usually strive for a Win-Lose, Lose-Win, or, worst of all, Lose-Lose philosophy. Most poor relationships can be categorized as a Lose-Lose scenario in that they are not gaining anything of value from their social circles, and neither are those people deriving anything of benefit from the relationship. In the end, you have millions of people actively engaged in social interactions that waste time and energy. This is why entire communities may become poor from one generation to another without anyone breaking the vicious circle to do something meaningful that will change the narrative. A Win-Win attitude is a mutually beneficial relationship attitude. Under this situation, you make progress, and I make progress; you add value to me, and I add value to you; you complement my weaknesses while I also complement yours. This is how mutually beneficial relationships work. When people only want to gain from you without contributing anything to you, they become nothing less than parasites out to destroy you. But someone may say, "I am poor; how can I add value to someone who is already influential? Why wouldn't that person help me to come out of my predicament so that I can help others?" The fact is that in the real world, nothing goes for nothing. And I think this is one of the foundational problems of poor people and why many of them remain perpetually poor and end up resenting rich people for what they often term 'greed' or 'selfishness.' To think that you must be rich or have something vital before being in a mutually beneficial relationship is one of the most significant lies of all time. Let me give you a practical example. I do a lot of free teaching on my social media handles to give back to the community and add value to others. Before making my teachings to this book, I taught on most of the ideas on my social media for free.

"To think that you must be rich or have something essential before you can be in a mutually beneficial relationship is one of the greatest lies of all times."

If you have been following me on any of my social media, I always ask my audience to help share my videos ten times, twenty times, fifty times, and so forth. The reason I do so is twofold. First, so that the value I am sharing may reach many people and benefit them. Second, it is my way of teaching you to reciprocate the weight I give you. Let me state a simple, known fact here: Sharing a video on social does not cost anything. But guess what? Most people who watch or listen to my videos usually refuse to share them despite many pleas for them to do so throughout the videos. Isn't it mind boggling that people will consume your content for free but intentionally refuse to share it with others even after pleading with them? How can such people who refuse to do something so little that will cost them nothing expect to cultivate mutually beneficial relationships with rich people? It is all about the mindset.

" Until you adopt a Win-Win attitude in your relationships, you are bound to remain stagnant or backward in your socio-economic state."

Most people who refuse to share videos with others despite knowing that doing so will not contribute anything significant to me erroneously think that if they share my content, they stand to lose while I stand to gain. But in reality, sharing free content that you find beneficial online is a Win-Win situation. Until you adopt a Win-Win attitude in your relationships, you are bound to remain stagnant or backward in your socio-economic state. Do you want to become a billionaire? Then start thinking of how to add value to others and derive value from them. Think Win-Win.

iii. They own multiple businesses but focus on one

While poor people own just one business, billionaires own multiple businesses and focus on one. Do you know that Bill Gates owns more than 100 businesses? One is like a significant business. Billionaires concentrate on that one until they have the most important breakthrough. The primary business becomes their signature business, and everyone knows who they are because of it. After that, however, they invest in several other companies. Bill Gates owns roughly 60% of First Season and several other companies, but most people only know him as the founder of Microsoft.

The first habit of billionaires is that they own multiple businesses; they do not put all their eggs in one basket. For example, Elon Musk started with PayPal; he was just one of ten co-founders. Elon Musk and his partners sold PayPal for two billion dollars. That was how he got his significant capital to start Tesla, then SpaceX, and he is investing in Bitcoin now.

Because poor people know that billionaires have multiple businesses, they also make the mistake of running various businesses. Owning and running are different things. Billionaires own numerous companies, but they only run one.

Jeff Bezos is back as one of the wealthiest men in the world after resigning from Amazon. When asked what else he wants to do, he said he wants to focus on all the other smaller businesses he owns. But poor people run everything simultaneously and don't even have enough staff. An average poor man who claims to be a business owner has blood pressure because he doesn't trust anyone.

"Don't chase everything simultaneously and end up losing everything."

A friend once came to me for a business talk, and I referred him to Gtext Homes to talk with them about the financial aspect. He felt I should be able to tell him as his friend, but I replied that I have people in charge of my financial affairs and that if I focused on the amount of money that enters my business, I would drop dead. So I have put structures in place, and they are running. That is how billionaires do it. But poor people chase everything at the same time.

Even in a job where a poor man is paid reasonably, he still looks for other small businesses, does not focus on where he is being paid, and ends up losing the job. These are mistakes that people make.

Dangote owns many businesses but is not in charge of many of them. The only one he is in order of is the refinery. All others have managing directors overseeing them. So billionaires get skilled people to take charge of their multiple businesses.

"Find investment opportunities that are trusted and can allow your money to work for you."

As an employee, focus on your job, make sure you're able to save a reasonable amount from what you're being paid, and find a way to set up a business that does not require that you run it. That's the way to keep your current job. Find investment opportunities that are trusted and can allow your money to work for you. Don't chase everything at the same time and end up losing everything.

iv. They surround themselves with Only Quality People

Another idea closely related to the Win-Win philosophy that is particularly important to imbibe is to practice Only Quality People (OQP). This idea was promulgated by the world-renowned motivational speaker Les Brown. According to Brown, one attitude for success is practising OQP. The concept of OQP entails relating, interacting, and associating only with people tested and proven reliable, valuable, and relatable. This is one of the secret habits of Billionaires. If you must create wealth and acquire riches, you must learn to weed off people who do not contribute anything meaningful to you. What benefits are there in relating with people who are always whining, gossiping, castigating others, and wasting your precious time with negative talks about others or specific societal events?

"If you must create wealth and acquire riches, you must learn to weed off people who do not contribute anything meaningful to you."

After meeting or talking with such people, you realize that no value is added to you. Instead, you feel drained emotionally and spiritually

"The kind of people you want to surround yourself with are those who win; you win; when they make progress, you also make progress."

because someone has succeeded in polluting your mind with negativity, the earlier you cut off such people from your life, the better it would be for you. You must embrace this philosophy and stand by it. If they cannot add value to your life, move on, never turn back, and never feel guilty about it. The kind of people you want to surround yourself with are those who win; when they make progress, you also make progress. Therefore, you must be determined to cut off people who are always telling you, "Please help me," "Please save me," "Please change my life," or "If you don't help me, I will die." Such people do not mean well to you. If you play into their chicaneries and subterfuges, you may discover your mistake when it is too late.

Generally, such people are alarmists who try to manipulate you by appealing to your emotions to see that their situation is dire and make you feel guilty if you refuse to do their bidding. You must learn to discern such people and resist them. They do not fit into the category of OQP. Such people are better referred to as OPP (Only Poor People). One of the ways to overcome the pressures OPP will want to put on you is always to remind them that everyone has a problem. And that is a fact. You also have many issues that you are seeking solutions to. Isn't that what life is all about? We are all seeking a solution to improve our lives; as we say in Nigeria, "*Wahala no dey finish*" (Trouble doesn't end). Such people must understand that everybody has a problem they are trying to solve or overcome. You have to be serious with the idea that anytime you are going into a relationship with someone, you are determined to add value to them, and most importantly, you are sure they are people who will add value to you. Let me share two real-life stories to buttress this point.

The first story concerns Pastor E. A. Adeboye (popularly known as Daddy G.O.), the General Overseer of the Redeemed Christian Church of God (RCCG). He once preached at the Redemption Camp and said, "My son died." Since no one had heard of such a misfortune befalling the famous man of God, people were immediately startled and stupefied. Since such large gatherings always involve an interpreter who interprets Daddy G.O.'s messages from English to Yoruba, the interpreter on this occasion thought that Daddy G. O. had made a mistake, and so instead of analysing what he had said, he decided to keep quiet with the hope that someone would correct the error. So, Daddy G. O. had to repeat it. This time he said, "I said my son died." Given this scenario, the interpreter reluctantly and, most probably, fearfully interpreted the message. As if that was not enough, Daddy G. O. said, "This my son is so dear to me. Every time I am in the United Kingdom, he comes around to handle my laundry, plan my itinerary, arrange my food, and do many other things to help me." He continued, "The last time I was in the United Kingdom, he was in a hospital bed. I visited him to pray for him, and he was concerned about who would take care of me. Even while on a

"...billionaires are not lazy; they just understand that the concept of being a business owner demands that your business can run without you."

hospital bed, he spoke with one of his friends and instructed him to help me. I looked at him and told him he should not be concerned about my welfare, my desire and prayer for him is to be well." I am sure that you

V. They make use of OPT

This is the principle by which your business can run without you. O.P.T. means other people's time. Billionaires use this to continue to build massive wealth. On the other hand, poor people must do all of the business because they have not discovered a way to automate.

"Create structures that use other people's time to automate your business."

I have not been in Nigeria for the last three months, but our company continues to open new estates. This month alone, three new estates were launched without my presence in Nigeria. That's the habit of billionaires. They create structures that use other people's time to automate their business. So, their businesses run with or without them.

By the way, billionaires are not lazy; they understand that the concept of being a business owner demands that your business can run without you.

Poor people do self-employment and call it owning a business. There's a difference. In self-employment, without you, the company can't run. But when you own a business, the industry is structured to run when you're not even there.

So many poor people quit their job with the excuse of being overused by their boss, only to start their own business and discover the whole stress is on them and they are getting sicker. They then realize how difficult it is to run a business.

I tell people that if you're going to have your own business, you better be your boss's best friend because you want to know how he got there, how he thinks, and his principles. If you want to be a billionaire, get a billionaire mentor.

2016 was the year I started listening to billionaires' advice on how to become a billionaire. I was shocked that becoming a billionaire is easier than becoming a millionaire. We are not saying you're a millionaire or billionaire by gift. If someone gives you a million dollars, you're not a millionaire. You're a millionaire if you understand how to run a business from scratch and generate income consistently to the tune of a billion or million. It's easier to be a billionaire than a millionaire because all that you need is based on

"Can you leave your business for six months and return to find it still running?"

principles. The key is having a mentor at that level who can help you scale. A mentee met me and learned how to do E-commerce. In six months, he earned over one hundred million naira. Right now, the business is almost gone. I remember telling him to be firm and build a structure, not just a product. He mastered the art of selecting the right product from me, but he needed to learn how to build a business. He didn't erect the proper templates and structures that could make the business run without him. He thought he could rely on his marketing skills, rent an office, and employ delectable ladies. They ran the whole thing down. One of them was stealing from him.

There is a difference between products and businesses. Investors don't invest in products; they invest in the business. Can you leave your business for six months and return to find it still running?

"Investors don't invest in products; they invest in the business."

That is how to know if you have a business. My mentee got married and moved to Abuja while the company was in Lagos, and it ran down. He didn't have a business structure, just a product.

6.   **Billionaires Scale Up Their Businesses with OPM After**

Gaining Social Capital:

OPM means Other People's Money. Many poor people start raising money for their businesses even before starting them. Billionaires don't do that. Microsoft, Tesla, and Uber went to the capital market after they got social capital. Even in Africa, everyone understood Dangote's business before he went public.

These are the mistakes we make. The poor man would say things like, "Dr. Stephen, if you can give me a million dollars, you'd see that I'm a good

"But truly, nobody can scale up a business without using other people's money."

businessman." No! That's not how it should be done. It would help if you first used whatever you know to test run and grow the business, demonstrate the value of the company, gain social capital, and then you can use other people's money. But honestly, nobody can scale up a business without using other people's money.

If Dangote's business fails to make a profit, would anyone blame Dangote for it? No. Nobody would call him a scammer. But you've not demonstrated if the business would work, and you've already started collecting money, taking loans, and others. At some point, if the company fails, people will go after you and call you a scammer. They will say you stole their money and that you're a fraud.

"I never started raising capital for our real estate company until we successfully ran the business for three years in the real estate sector."

You're not supposed to start raising capital until you've demonstrated that the business would work and that you know what you're doing. I never started raising money for our real estate company until we'd successfully run the business for three years in the real estate sector. I have now built a structure as a multi-billion naira real estate company in Africa. So, nobody will say we are scammers if we raise 50 billion naira to expand our real estate projects. It took time to build the company into a household name. We were on TV with CNN, Channels Television, our Rolls Royce show, AIT, etc. Now, we can go for other people's money.

Famous examples of Billionaire entrepreneurs

Some global billionaire entrepreneurs, according to Forbes, are:

i. Bernard Arnault and his family
ii. Elon Musk
iii. Jeff Bezos
iv. **Gautam Adani**
v. **Bill Gates**
vi. Warren Buffet
vii. Larry Ellison
viii. Larry Page
ix. Steve Ballmer
x. Carlos Slim

Lifestyle and net worth

i. Elon Musk

With a net worth of more than $219 Billion, Elon Musk is estimated to be one of the world's richest man. He's the CEO of Tesla, a clear thinker and communicator, and always hires people who: avoid long and frequent meetings; embrace failure (he believes if you are afraid of failing, you can't create innovative products); embrace change; and are optimistic.

ii. Jeff Bezos

Jeff Bezos is the second-richest man in the world, with an estimated net worth of $187 billion. He is the Founder of the E-commerce giant called Amazon.

Jeff Bezos's leadership principles are: be obsessed with your customers; take risks; invent and embrace failure; think long term and be patient; make your team agile; take high-quality decisions; and don't use presentation slides during meetings.

iii. Bernard Arnault

Having a net worth of $158 billion, Bernard Arnault oversees the LVMH empire of about 70 fashion and cosmetics brands, including the famous Louis Vuitton and Sephora.

iv. Bill Gates

Bill Gates is the third, with an estimated net worth of $97 billion. He is the founder of Microsoft Corporation and is credited with revolutionizing the PC industry with Windows. He has been fascinated by coding since an early age.

His leadership principles are: failure is a great teacher; empower others; learn from unhappy customers; don't underestimate change; and give back to charity.

v. Warren Buffet

Warren Buffet, the owner of Berkshire Hathaway, is one of the most successful investors, with an estimated net worth of $82 billion. He is a humanitarian. Despite his billionaire status, he leads a simple lifestyle.

vi. Larry Ellison

Larry Ellison is the co-founder of software giant Oracle. He has an estimated net worth of $62 billion.

vii. Mark Zuckerberg

Mark Zuckerberg is the founder of Facebook. He has an estimated net worth of $62 billion. Facebook recently bought some social networks, like Instagram and WhatsApp. Despite his billionaire status, he leads a simple lifestyle.

CHAPTER TWO

HABIT 1: MAINTAINING JOY IN BUSINESS TRIALS

"Nothing lasts forever or stays the same, and you cannot be haunted forever.

In this chapter, I want us to look at the compelling subject of joy in trials and moderation in victories.

One thing I have seen that has led to depression and suicide is a lack of execution. Anytime you are on the verge of a breakthrough, it does not even make sense to be worried or sad. It doesn't make sense to be unhappy in your moment of trial because you are just about to hit something. After all, after the trial, what comes next? Victory.

Nothing lasts forever, nothing stays the same, and you cannot be haunted forever. So, at some point, you begin to enjoy the victory, and at some point, you begin to enjoy success. So the time you're facing trials and challenges should be the time you're jubilating and excited because the next thing that will come after that is victory and success. So, therefore, learn to jubilate and be joyful during times of crises; let that be when you say, "Thank you, Lord!"

On the flip side of this conversation, when you succeed, be moderate in your victory.

Many people don't know how to be moderate because when you win, you should prepare for the next battle, the next feat, and you should understand that there will soon be another trying time, and I just won this battle.

We have in Billionaire Habits for Entrepreneurs: joy in trials and moderation in victory. The victory allows you to gather momentum and energy for the next battle, which is one of my biggest strengths.

I build momentum for my next battle during my victories, so I'm very moderate when I'm victorious; I'm very reasonable when I've won; I'm very mild, and the reason why I'm moderate is not that I'm not happy; it's not even because I'm scared; it's because I'm preparing for the next challenge.

The next challenge will inevitably happen; it's just how the world works. I remember when I got married, and it coincided with when I faced the most difficult challenges in my business. It wasn't easy, and I'll never forget my wife coming to me. In Africa, you must get your parent's consent before you get married. In that case, my father-in-law said he wasn't interested in having his daughter marry me, and his concern was that I would be abusive.

I remember the day I met him; he kept asking me, "Where are you from?" He was curious if I had anyone notable in my immediate family. In Africa, if you give your daughter in marriage, you're technically giving her to a family, so you want to know who the important people in the husband's family are—whether they are people with a reputation or people you can hold accountable if something goes wrong. There was nobody; I didn't have anyone in my lineage, and my wife insisted on marrying me. Can you imagine that? I was the one who suffered because she forced me to commit a crime. I broke up the relationship after three months. Finally, I said, "You know what, if your dad is not going to have me, let's go our separate ways." My wife insisted, "It's either you or nobody else," so we went ahead and married.

Afterwards, it seemed almost as if something spiritual happened: I lost everything I had; I couldn't renew our office space; businesses shut down the products we were selling; our partners cancelled their contracts with us; those who had already committed to helping people study abroad cancelled it; people asked for refunds of money we didn't have, among other happenings. During this time, I learned many business lessons because we had already told them there was no refund, but it was not written in any document, and some of them started causing trouble.

I wondered if it was because of what we did that we were suffering, going through all these difficult times, and I remembered telling my wife, "You need to stop thinking like this because we are about to get a breakthrough, and when we finally had a breakthrough, nothing could bring us down." Right, as I said, we're going through a difficult time, but we should be happy because we're about to make a breakthrough, and after that, nothing else can happen; the next step is inevitable: rising to the top!

The next point at this point is to go up, so I remember saying to her, "We are about to go up, and it's going to be big, and this time around, we will go up; we are not coming down again." (laughs)

"It is wisdom, ladies and gentlemen, to take yourself up, brace yourself, and let yourself know that joy should come at this moment of trial because I'm about to break through, I'm about to break forth, and there is something big that's about to happen."

And today, after many years? It's been nine years, and that's what happened: we ascended and did not descend. So, rather than succumbing to depression, looking for someone to blame, despise, or hold accountable for some of your challenges, take things in stride!

It is wisdom, ladies and gentlemen, to take yourself up, brace yourself, and let yourself know that joy should come at this moment of trial because I'm about to break through, I'm about to break forth, and there is something big that's about to happen. As an entrepreneur, you will face numerous challenges in your business; you will run out of liquidity, and if you're in construction or real estate like I am, you may run out of money, and all your sites will be closed down. However, rejoice because you are about to make a breakthrough; you may have many products and build all these properties all over the place.

"The time of victory is the time for moderation; it's the time to be moderate because there will be a tougher season..."

I visited a property site some time ago, and you could see that they had slowed down construction because they had run out of cash. This particular developer bought six islands out of the world's total, and they've built some of the most iconic buildings there, but you'll see that construction has slowed down due to liquidity. But now is the time to be optimistic because there will be a breakthrough; something will happen for you, and it's critical that you live your life with that kind of mindset. It's darkest before dawn, and one should be joyful because something big is about to happen.

So, even if you're not sure what to do next, be joyful because something big is about to happen—something extraordinary, glorious, fabulous, and magnificent; that's the attitude, that's the mindset, even if you're not sure what to do next. I've seen stories of people committing suicide because they lacked a balanced mindset.

The time of victory is the time for moderation; it's the time to be moderate because there will be a more arduous season, and I should use my time of victory to prepare for my next battle.

I've seen many people waste their moments of victory; they squander them away; they act as though there won't be another moment of battle; they behave as though everything will always be good. Unfortunately, that is not the case.

CHAPTER THREE

HABIT 2: PRACTICE MODERACY IN VICTORY

Lessons From Elon Musk

"Life is good and bad; bad in itself is not evil; it's necessary to keep us humble."

Life is good and bad; bad in itself is not evil; it's necessary to keep us humble. Your moment of crisis is also your moment of humility, and life is a mix of victories and battles, victories and challenges. And in your moment of triumph, be moderate. Sit down, reminisce, sit down, and think. When I make my most significant sales, sometimes the most money in my life, I sit down for a week for the next moment of battle and put structures in place so that the next time I have a credit crunch, I'll have enough support; I've built enough systems, but you won't know, and that's one of the biggest secrets.

Let me give you an example. How many of you know Elon Musk is financially in his most demanding season? You should know that I'm not sure Elon Musk has ever borrowed and sold his Tesla shares the way he had to do in a year, 2022. Instead, he has sold more Tesla shares than ever; he has had to borrow money and borrowed a lot of it to buy Twitter. As a result, he needs more money this season than at any other time in his life.

People like that have built a system where you'll hardly ever know when a Billionaire is poor or rich. It's almost like he's in the same state all the time, and the reason it looks that way is because of systems and structures that have been put in place during the time of plenty. So, in times of plenty, billionaires will first have a plan that ensures they are never personally affected by their company's financial struggles. Never. And this is a very sound financial foundation; you must put that structure in place.

CHAPTER FOUR

HABIT 3: CREATING A STRUCTURE OF PERSONAL INCOME PROTECTION

"Have a structure that protects your income."

Your company going through a tough time should not mean you can't pay your bills; that would amount to a crazy life.

"You must separate personal finances from company funds."

So, you must have a structure that protects your income. Because you are different from your company, you must separate personal finances from company funds. Your company and yourself must be well separated. Unfortunately, many entrepreneurs don't have that proper separation and balance between themselves and their companies.

CHAPTER FIVE

HABIT 4: CREATING A STRATEGY OF EXECUTION DURING TOUGH SEASONS

"People don't hate you; they just hate some of your ideas, your guts, and are not sure why they hate you."

It would help if you had a strategy to execute during the difficult season, as you saw when Elon Musk bought Twitter. Twitter was using how much—was it 4 million dollars every day? It's okay for you to start doing that; it's not an emotion. Emotion has no place in business. Business is not sentiment; you need to cut down. You'll hear that some people will be fired and that some people will be unhappy, but this is only for a short time. If you eventually execute all of the plans and the company becomes highly profitable, gets back on the street, and becomes big again, everyone will still come back and call you a genius. We are never stable with our opinions, so don't take them personally. People don't hate you; they hate some of your ideas and guts and are not sure why they hate you.

I remember a young man posted on my Facebook page, saying, "I have never met this Dr Stephen, but I just don't like him." And I replied, "Sorry, there are some days that I'm not sure I like myself too." It's okay; it's your opinion, and you're entitled to it, but I'm not going to convince myself that I'm a terrible person because some person doesn't like me, right? I'm not even sure you enjoy yourself that much; you don't necessarily hate me; you're executing what you do to yourself. So, when people don't like you, they're technically saying they don't like themselves; but expressing what they are probably doing to themselves. They probably don't like themselves that much, and if you take it personally, if you say, "Oh, he doesn't like me, no, says who?" He doesn't like himself either.

"Be consistent, even when you don't feel like it."

That is not personal, and so for me, in that moment of victory, what wealthy people have done is put structures in place, put a system in place that will help sustain them when the weather changes again because it will change. That is just the way the world is wired. Good, deficient, yin, yang, positive, negative—that's how the world works. Nobody hates you; the world is just not always fixed, and you must understand this dimension and live your life with the understanding that you must structure your life in such a way that when things are working or not working, you are stable, constant, consistent, and resilient. So I've prepared myself to overcome this next challenge, and the good news is that it's only a matter of time before everything changes and everything turns around for the better. But you must have that staying stamina; you must have the energy to withstand the most demanding season of your life; you must build that stamina, okay?

"Be consistent, even when you don't feel like it."

Be consistent, even when you don't feel like it. Be consistent, even when things don't go your way.

Structure things in this way, and that's why I'm not angry or sad that Elon Musk has to downsize this way; I understand! He'd done it to Tesla and other of his businesses as well. Right, there's a season, a phase, that you have to cut back on, and you better cut back on time, so you don't get completely swallowed up during the phase, cut down on time.

I remember sharing this with crypto investors when everything was booming when bitcoin hit over $50,000, and everyone was excited and jubilant: "Oh, go buy bitcoin; do you have bitcoin?" Have you got a Bitcoin? And I remember

"You spend less when you have money, and you spend more when you

have less."

saying in a Tiktok video, "Go sell your bitcoin now," and not everyone believed me; some said I was crazy; who tells anybody to sell bitcoin at a time when bitcoin has hit the highest amount ever? Dr Stephen Akintayo tells you to do so; those who didn't listen to me then didn't sell their bitcoin. Well, bitcoin is less than 10 thousand dollars now.

If you didn't sell when it was high, you're probably out of money right now, ladies and gentlemen. And I've shared this rule with you many times: *when they zig you zag, and when they zag you zig.* Don't always behave like everyone else; always take the opposite direction. So, for example, we get to downsize, but guess what, we're going to expand aggressively in 2023. We are going to reduce to develop. So we pushed ourselves for an unusual expansion and wanted to broaden our asset base through asset acquisition rights to purchase properties and other assets without incurring overhead. But we will expand heavily in that same year of recession, and, like you have never seen before, you're going to see us taking bold steps.

We have already announced 1,000 housing units in 2023; we may even do more than 1,000 housing units in 2023, which is the level of expansion, but we have prepared for the moment of victory and success; and in times of crisis, we can think big and expand bigger; that's how you play this game.

Dear Entrepreneur, you have to play this game in times of crisis; when things are tough, you should think of an expansion; when your business is facing a difficult time, you should negotiate and plan your next business move.

Even when your business is doing well, you should be cautious. You spend less when you have money, and you spend more when you have less. Here is my

"It's because principles and philosophy are not normal; they are not

regular!"

view: If we'd done things the way everybody else has done, we would have gotten what others have brought. It's because principles and philosophy are not standard; they are not regular. That's why we are where we are today, and that's why we have come this far.

If you can practice what others are not doing, you'll get what others are not getting. You have to know that you cannot do things the way others are doing them and get their kind of result; no, you have to do

"If you can practice what others are not doing, you'll get what others are not getting."

things in a different, unusual way, and experience things. That is how these things work.

CHAPTER SIX

HABIT 5: GIVING

"The giving concept of capitalism is to build to the top before giving."

In this chapter, we will look at the habit of giving. What I have realized about billionaires and wealthy people is their crazy giving culture.

Until recently, wealthy people did not publicly announce their charitable contributions, which began with charities, foundations, etc.

The media believe that wealthy people don't give, and it's false.

Let me start with John D. Rockefeller. He was the first American billionaire; by the time he was 51, he had already given 50 per cent of his earnings to charity. The Rockefeller Foundation is still one of the most prominent charity organizations in the world. Jeff Bezos does the same. He even said he would give all his earnings to charity.

Now let me start with the concept:

The giving idea of capitalism is to build to the top before giving.

Many people have tried the reverse, and it didn't turn out very well because they were trying to play god at the inception of their business. It's like a rocket launcher: it requires much force to shoot up. So many people know this, so before giving to charity, get to the top.

I'll also share some of the other billionaires that give as well.

Andrew Carnegie, at one point, owned half of America's railroads, and he practised this concept of giving too. He had a board meeting where he told his

"If I am going to give, I don't want to encourage laziness; it has to be empowering."

Employees needed to start teaching people how they made it to the top. He even sponsored some motivational speakers to teach people how to make money.

I practice these things too, but I make sure my giving doesn't make people lazy. If I am going to give, I don't want to encourage laziness; it has to be empowering.

"I make sure my giving doesn't make people lazy."

For example, I frequently receive messages saying, "Please help me sponsor my wedding, naming ceremony, and all that." I am not God, and I am not Jesus Christ. I didn't die for the sins of the world; Jesus did.

So, if I'm going to give, it has to encourage empowerment rather than laziness; that's one of the reasons we have the book, Billionaire Habits for Pastors. You should read it too. This is because sometimes pastors encourage this. God gave the children of the Israelites manna in the wilderness, not in Canaan, so at some point, God will make you responsible as you grow, but that doesn't mean you should sit back and keep saying God will do everything. It encourages laziness.

Any faith that encourages idleness has failed. That is why our spiritual leaders must teach these things, whether a Pastor, Imam, or Rabbi. We need to teach people these things so they won't depend on us for survival.

My charities are structured. I remember someone sending a photo to my page (this is why my team blocks specific individuals most time). She sent me a photo of her breast cancer, and I was not mentally sane for three days. If I'm not mentally sane, how will I help you?

That's why every charity has to be structured. Again, we will be giving out 5 million dollars to SMEs in the coming years. It has been structured. I don't

"Put a structure in place so that it will still be running even when you're dead."

know who gets what. I've already arranged for professionals to be in charge of that. That is why you should put structures in place if you run a charity. Our charity is registered in both Nigeria and the US. And tax is not deductible.

My scholarship program is also well-organized. Every year, we give a certain amount from my real estate sales, books, and mentoring books and programs.

If you don't put structures in place for your charity, people will emotionally blackmail you, especially if you come from certain parts of the world. And you may end up giving your money to the wrong people, who don't need it but have formed the habit of begging, thereby depriving the right people. So put a structure in place so that it will still be running even when you're dead.

"If you don't put structures in place for your charity, people will emotionally blackmail you."

Those SMEs we will be helping will also actually give back to our charity organization from the earnings they will make as well.

I started my charity with about 13–15 people, and we all contributed around 3,000 naira at the time, went to an orphanage, bought things for them, taught them soccer, acting, etc. My charity even started before my business. When my staff meet for the morning devotion, we encourage them to give. Start giving from where you are.

Billionaires are not called so because of the money they have in their accounts, but by the assets they own. One of the wealthiest man, Elon Musk, dropped from being so after selling his shares and even borrowing money from the bank to buy Twitter.

"Giving is a universal principle that guarantees success and the multiplication of one's fortunes."

If you are a Christian, you should be aware that the Bible states that whoever gives to the poor lends to the Lord. Sometimes I even give; it's due to a pledge. For example, when we sell housing units, I put money into them with the expectation of profit.

These are some habits that have helped us grow.

The richest man is not calculated by account balance. Some people, when they hear the word "Billionaire," think it's due to the person's account balance. However, Forbes and other organizations don't operate that way. Instead, they calculate your assets to determine who the wealthiest man is.

Some people will say, "Oh, billionaires don't have problems; they don't even know what to do with money." On the contrary, billionaires even need more money than they do. Money hardly stays in their account. It goes into projects, and they need more money than anyone.

Start the giving culture. Remember the biblical story of the widow who gave? She was the one who contributed the most.

"Start giving at your level!"

Giving is a universal principle that guarantees success and the multiplication of one's fortunes. That can be referred to as the "benevolence principle." Billionaires understand this principle and engage in many forms of charity and philanthropy. They know that their wealth increases to a reasonable extent on their giving.

"Giving is a universal principle that guarantees success and the multiplication of one's fortunes."

Let me share a powerful anecdote to expound on this claim. It is about how I got my first substantial financial breakthrough. Six years ago, the church I attended organized a 21-day prayer and fasting program at the beginning of the new year, and I joyfully participated in the program. After the period of prayer and fasting, our pastor told us that he felt led to ask us to empty the money in our bank accounts and send it to the founder of our church. He said some of us willing to obey this injunction would experience unique breakthroughs. But he did not provide any information beyond that.

Let's face it: From a natural and logical standpoint, such an injunction does not make sense. How can you ask people to take everything they have and send it to someone who already has a good life? But guess what? For some reasons that could only be understood in hindsight, I was "foolish" enough to obey the instruction. I cashed out the twenty five thousand naira in my account—all I had at the time—and put it in the offering, that was on a Sunday morning. That was when I was still struggling to build my bulk SMS company.

Monday morning, I received a call from a company that wanted me to supply bulk SMS to them to the tune of thirty million naira. To say that I was astounded and, at the same time, perplexed would be an understatement. I thought that someone was playing a prank on me. To compound the situation, the voice on the phone sounded like that of a child. But because I have learned never to despise anyone, I consented to the request and went ahead and sent an invoice to the company.

Before that time, the most prominent business order I had ever received was for two million naira. But suddenly, there was an invoice for thirty million naira. By Tuesday morning, I got a call from the company to inform me that they were ready to pay the money into my bank account. And shortly after that call, I received an alert from my bank about their deposit of the said amount. But

"Billionaires become richer by giving."

because my bank had never seen such a transaction in my account history, they had to freeze my account and interrogate me to be sure. In the end, they were convinced to allow me to use the money for my business purposes.

In short, that was my significant financial breakthrough in life. From that point on, my life and business changed for the better. Isn't it amazing how a single incident can change a person's life forever?

But why did I recount this somewhat personal religious experience? It is not to try to convert anyone to my church or to make any statement about Christianity specifically. This anecdote is meant to make the case that giving is a universal principle that constantly works under every circumstance when used appropriately. And this is one of the ways billionaires multiply their money. In the end, billionaires become more prosperous by giving.

The late M. K. O. Abiola, a former Nigerian business magnate and politician, once illustrated that "the giving hand is always on top." By that, he meant that the benevolent person will always be ahead of those who do not give; since he gives, the laws of the universe work to see that he stays atop to continue giving to those below. This is one of the powerful principles that billionaires use to continue to become more prosperous and multiply their wealth. Because of their benevolence, billionaires are always ahead of the people they help.

"Benevolence does not only open you up to the world; it also enhances and multiplies your influence and resources."

The African Union recently gave Tony Elumelu a diplomatic passport that allows him to visit all parts of Africa without a visa. He was granted the same travel privileges on a Caribbean Island. How did Elumelu earn those privileges while many other billionaires in Africa who are much richer than him have not been given them? The answer is obvious: It is because of his many benevolent acts. The Tony Elumelu Foundation is involved in many acts of charity across the African continent. The African Union (AU), knowing the impact that the Tony Elumelu Foundation has been making on the continent, decided to grant him a diplomatic passport so that he can continue to travel freely in all parts of Africa without any restrictions. The AU sees Elumelu as a true African representative because of his foundation's diverse acts of benevolence and philanthropy. It is not surprising that Elumelu hosts webinars for heads of state in Africa because of their respect and trust for him. These are some of the advantages of benevolence.

Benevolence opens you up to the world and enhances and multiplies your influence and resources. In technical terms, this is referred to as "social capital." Social capital means "the networks of relationships among people who live and work in a particular society, enabling that society to function effectively." It follows that the one who is rich in benevolence is also rich in social capital.

"Benevolence does not only open you up to the world; it also enhances and multiplies your influence and resources."

Giving helps you gain social capital, and social capital opens you up to the world. It builds strong networks of relationships that give you easy access to prominent and influential people. Because of the philanthropic gestures of Elumelu, presidents of African countries beg him to come to their countries and improve their people's lives through his foundation's various initiatives. Elumelu has easy access to places where others must go through lengthy procedures due to his solid social capital base.

This universal principle is always at work. Adam M. Grant, an American psychologist and professor of organizational management at the prestigious Wharton Business School of the University of Pennsylvania, has conducted extensive research on giving and receiving. In his bestselling book, "Give and Take: A Revolutionary Approach to Success," Grant shows that "added to hard work, talent, and luck, highly successful people need the ability to connect with others." The book also explains that "givers give more than they get, takers get more than they give, and matchers aim to give and get equally; all can succeed." But the book's significant contribution is its assertion that "generous people do better at work than selfish ones." Contrary to widely held opinions, Grant demonstrates that people who are generous and kind toward others finish first.

Billionaires get richer by giving. Some people think that most billionaires give because they are friendly people. The truth is that they give from the perspective of expanding their social capital globally, which helps them expand their businesses and multiply their income. Such acts of philanthropy and benevolence may even serve as a way to make their businesses grow faster.

I was encouraged to buy from my real estate company because they recognized that I have a foundation and do much charity. For instance, the Stephen Akintayo Foundation pays tuition fees for orphans and helps people displaced by ethnoreligious crises and forced to live in IDP camps. Because people see and know about my foundation's charity, benevolence, and philanthropy, they know that if they buy from my company, some of the money will go into the foundation and help those in need. In doing so, they also feel that they are indirectly contributing to helping others by merely buying

"Giving is living!"

from my company. I am permanently moved to hear such submissions from some of our customers.

Giving is one of the ways billionaires get wealthier. So, when people often tell me that rich people don't give, I laugh. I laugh because such people do not understand that giving is one of the things that makes billionaires richer. Have you ever wondered why many celebrities, famous people, and billionaires are always involved in one form of philanthropy or another? It is because such acts showcase them to the world as good and kind people and invariably help open more doors and opportunities for them.

Some billionaires prefer to give privately, while others do it publicly. But it doesn't matter whether the giving is done in private or in public. People get to hear about it. Most billionaires have annual budgets for charity and philanthropy. They do so because they understand that giving has multiple benefits. It is impossible to be a true giver and not receive multiple returns. Try giving if you want an easy and faster route to multiplying your income and wealth.

Giving is living. The benevolent individual understands the principles of a happy and fulfilling life. Giving is a powerful instrument that has been shown to increase self-esteem and life expectancy.

There are three levels of giving. The first step is to give it to your parents. I have just completed the construction of a house for my father. While it is a small house, my father is proud that his son built him a house. Although I cannot recall my father ever paying my tuition (my mother was the one who worked hard to pay our school fees!), he nevertheless played his part well in providing moral and spiritual training that has helped me to be where I am today, and I am forever grateful for that. Whether he took financial care of me is not the most important thing. I appreciate the fact that he was always there for me. Because he is my father, he deserves my respect and gratitude. And the way to show him gratitude is to take care of his basic needs. Therefore, I send him money every month to take care of himself.

Even before I became rich, I knew and understood the importance of caring for my parents. Before my mother died, I did not have much, but I tried to help her with the bit of business I did while on the university campus. I remember buying her a wristwatch after we did a trade fair, which happened to be the first business I had ever engaged myself in. After that business, I thought that because my mother sacrificed so much for us, it was ideal to buy her something as a token of appreciation. That act remains one of the things I am most proud of today. I had no idea she wasn't going to live very long. My mother was my heroin and breadwinner, but she died young. She died while still paying my university tuition. The little I could do for her before her demise still brings me joy today, even though she did not live long enough to benefit from my financial prosperity.

I wanted to do something little for my mother before she died. She died while I was in my final year at the university. If I had waited for the right time to help, I wouldn't have done anything for her because she did not live long enough to witness my financial prosperity. After her death, I decided to adopt two women, to whom I am not related, as my mothers. I did that because I respect them and look up to them to fill that vacuum in my life. For my adopted mothers, I do send them some money every month to help with their upkeep. The financial support I give them may not be much, but it is essential because they have always been there for me.

"Give it to your parents and watch how your life will improve."

Sometimes people misunderstand the purpose of giving. They think of giving in terms of the volume of what is given, not the motive. But giving is not so much about the volume as the goal. It does not matter how much you have; you can send your parents something consistent every month. There is something magical about giving to parents. It expands and increases you beyond measure because of the parental blessings that will keep pouring on you. Give it to your parents and watch how your life will improve. It is not about volume. Just make sure that you send them something consistently, no matter how small. Sacrifices made for one's parents pay off.

However, a word of caution is in order: do not spend all your money trying to help your parents. This is the other side of the coin that can cripple you financially. Make sure that you help your parents. But do not succumb to their unreasonable financial demands that can cripple you. My father once wanted to trick me through indirect emotional blackmail. He would tell me, "Son, people see you on social media and keep mocking me that my son is prospering while I am suffering." They think that the life you display on social media does not conform with the kind of life your father lives. I had to confront my father about such an attitude, frankly. It would be best if you were determined not to allow anyone to trick you into spending all your savings on your parents. You must be discreet and moderate about it to grow and help them better in the future. If I had listened to my father's complaints and spent all my savings helping him, I would not have grown financially to build a house for him later.

If you are a religious person and have people who are your pastors or imams or the leaders of any religion that you practice, you must learn to give to support such people because of their spiritual oversight over you. They pray for you and work hard to provide you with spiritual nourishment. Some of them not only pray for you, but they also fast. That is why it is crucial to make sure that you set aside something to support your spiritual mentors because of the spiritual covering they provide over your life.

"It is important to make sure that you set aside something to support your spiritual mentors because of the spiritual covering they provide over your life."

Some spiritual atmospheres can either take you up or bring you down. If someone plays an essential role in helping you spiritually, it is logical that you reciprocate by giving to that person. That is a powerful principle because the more you give them, even if they don't see you or talk about your specific giving, their spirit is praying for you. They constantly think about you and pray to God about your prosperity.

The third level of giving is to the poor. Many people in Africa erroneously think that only the rich are supposed to give, while the poor watch and applaud the benevolence of the rich. The person who needs to give more is the poor person because he is the one who needs more. Isn't that the reason we want more? Unfortunately, rich people seem to understand this principle more than poor people. While the rich keep giving and receiving tremendous amounts in return, the poor keep being miserly with their resources and becoming poorer by the day. I give more when I am broke because the whole concept of giving is to get more. For instance, why do farmers plant crops in the ground? It is because they want to have a bountiful harvest. But before they can have a bountiful harvest of the same crop, they must be willing to give some of it away. The same principle applies to giving. What does a poor person need? Money! But to have money, he must first be willing to give out his little. That does not sound logical, but it is the operational principle of wealth multiplication that billionaires and rich people use to amass more wealth.

All of my financial mentors are richer than i, but I keep contributing money to support their various endeavours. I do it for myself, not for them. For example, one of my mentors is a leadership expert. I have devoured most of his books over the years, and I can confidently say that his books are responsible for shaping my leadership skills and multiplying my income. Recently, I asked him to be a guest in one of my programs, and his workers sent me a bill for fifty thousand dollars for that guest appearance. While the amount sounded outrageous initially, when I paused to think about everything I have learned from him over the years, my hesitation in paying that amount immediately vanished. Rather than comparing his financial status with mine and whining about the amount of money his company was charging me, I focused on all the benefits I had enjoyed from his services and the multiplier effect that his presence in my program would have.

If you are poor, learn to give to people who are poorer than you. I started doing charity while I was still a student. My friends and I would go to orphanages and do projects for them. We were poor students when we started helping orphans and giving to the poor. My first charity project was for three thousand naira. I spoke with ten of my friends, and we decided to donate three thousand naira each to help people whose socioeconomic conditions were worse than ours. That was how we started. But see how far I have come. I didn't get here by chance. I understood the principle of giving and decided to put it into practice.

CHAPTER SEVEN

HABIT 6: GOAL SETTING

"All the billionaires I know are habitual goal setters."

I want us to look at the subject of the goal-setting habit. All the Billionaires that I know are dangerous goal-setters. They just set crazy goals, which is why some of the names that have been used to describe Billionaires include scammers and unrealistic people!

So, here's an example; I'm not even going to claim credit for this one; when I'm in Dubai, I live in the Burj Khalifa. I own an apartment there. My wife visited me here at the Burj Khalifa; she reminded me that the first time we visited the Burj, there was this experience where you go through Dubai Mall and use the elevator to get to the top of the Burj Khalifa, and she said I told her I'd be living here one day; that demonstrates the power of goal setting.

All the billionaires I know are habitual goal setters; I went a step further 14 years ago and made a 50-year goal plan, and you see why many people don't make progress. How many of you believe that the people who tell you that they don't believe in goal setting are mostly the ones who have not achieved anything tangible?

I remember interviewing somebody recently, and the person said, *"Oh, I don't believe in this pressure of goal setting,"* As sweet as it sounded, I looked at where she was, and I realized why she was not beyond where she had gotten to. I'm in the 14th year of my 50-year goal plan; without that setup, I wouldn't even know if I'm making progress. One of the most compelling reasons to set a goal is that it allows you to see how far you've come and how far you still have to go. It even helps you become grateful.

"You owe it to yourself to believe in your dreams!"

You live a life full of gratitude because you can see how far God has taken you. You said you wanted to do this and that, and I've also realized that people with goal setting habits are self-motivated. One of the best ways to become self-motivated is to develop goal-setting habits and set your own goals. So many of the wealthiest people in the world set goals for themselves. I want to do this; I want to achieve this by this year; I have this dream; I want to get this done. People who live their lives that way go far.

I remember somebody I met in, I think, 2012 or so, and he had this dream. He's a photographer, and today he's the official photographer of my president in Nigeria, but you could see him as a young man who had so many dreams. I remember meeting him, and as he shared some of the pictures he has taken, there was so much passion that you could tell this guy was going far.

Everyone I've seen who has made it in this world was someone who dared to set goals, someone who dared to dream, someone who dared to talk about what they were going to do, where they were going, what they wanted to achieve, and how they'd get there; they had these crazy ideas, and some people didn't believe them, but that's okay. Many thought I was crazy, and many called me all manner of names growing up, but I had the goal, not them; it was my goal, my dream. I'm the one.

"Everyone I've seen who has made it in this world was someone who dared to set goals, someone who dared to dream, someone who dared to talk about what they were going to do, where they were going, what they wanted to achieve, and how they'd get there...."

I was the ambitious one; I was the one with this incredible thing I wanted to become, not them.

So always remember: whenever people doubt your dream and goals, they are not the dreamer; you are! You owe it to yourself to believe in your dreams. I've met people, and they'd tell me how people don't believe in their dream, and I'm

"Goals live on as long as they are pursued!"

like, "It's your dream for Christ's sake, not theirs," so you owe it to yourself to believe in it so that it comes to pass.

Some people may tell you it's a lie; some may tell you it's a joke; others may tell you it won't work, but hey, people will always talk, right? People will always talk, and people will always doubt, especially those who have never done it before and especially those who aren't going very far; they will always doubt you, and they will always talk about you, but just because they have the right to an opinion doesn't make it right. People will say things like, "See how he talks; see how he moves; he's so arrogant; he's this; he's that" if you decide to be great or big. It's their opinion; you set your goals and pursue them.

You must talk about your goals. You know the story about Walt Disney, the man who started Disney World, and how he died before Disney World was commissioned, and how some of his friends were saying how they wished Disney was alive to see this Disney World and all of that, and the wife said to them that he saw it before you guys did, and you're just seeing what he saw then. He saw it, said it, and walked towards it, which is why dreams don't die.

Goals live on as long as they are pursued. So the initiators of great dreams and visions don't die; they can't die; they don't die at all; their dreams live on even when they leave this earth; the dream goes on; the dream pushes on; so the wife told them he saw the vision before you all did; you're just getting to see what he saw; so always remember that it's your dream, but for the dream to come to pass, you must talk about it.

They had not even finished the Burj Khalifa excavation when the developer said, "We're building the tallest building in the world." You know

"Every dreamer, every goal-setter is, first and foremost, a liar!"

what's funny about the Burj Khalifa? (And probably why I decided to say I want to live here.) The Alabar, who is the Emir's chairman, grew up in Dubai when there was no water and no electricity, and when he was talking about this project that would gulp Billions of dollars (they had not even begun excavation), he said they wanted to do something tall; they wanted to do the biggest, and when he spoke to the Sheikh, the Sheikh said if it's not big, we are not doing it. At some point, they ran into issues with finances, which is normal and is just part of the job, particularly in real estate; we're always running into financial issues where there's not enough to complete the project. The project was paused for almost a year because of money, but today it's a reality. The Burj Khalifa is here! They made it happen! People said it would never happen; they said Dubai was a scam; they said Dubai was deceiving people, but it is now a reality. Every dreamer and every goal-setter is, first and foremost, a liar! They will not be hailed until their dream comes true. Oh, what a wonderful man or woman! Wow! What an innovator! What an inventor! But what's funny is that they're praised by everyone, even those who call them liars.

People don't hate you; they just hate the idea you're perpetuating. They hate the concept. The same people who say they don't like you can come back tomorrow and say you're their role model, mentor, genius, and someone they look up to. It has happened to me many times.

I've seen people who said crazy things on social media later come back and say, "Sir, when I first met you, I didn't like you, but now I realize you're a great man," and I smile like if I took what you said too personally when you said it, and now you've come back apologizing, we'd still be enemies, but I never did.

I remember a young man who was in my office one day and said he used to know me when I was starting my business years ago, and he once called me a scammer and all kinds of other names (he was the one telling me all this), that he insulted me and was calling me to apologize, and that if he had known I would go this far, he wouldn't have said some of the things he said. And I remember saying to him, "You are more than forgiven; I can't even remember what you did when you did it, or how you did it," which was true. I honestly couldn't remember. So, this is why you shouldn't take some things too seriously or too personally; let the mockery be the fuel for your greatness. So when people are mocking you and telling you you're a liar, it's never going to happen because you don't have the resources and you don't have the skills to make it happen; nobody has ever done it; this is a scam; you're just deceiving people. Somebody once sent a letter to all my customers telling them not to believe in me, telling them all manner of things, but all he has just done is to fuel me up, to energize me, and to give me more reasons why, no matter what, we have to get this thing done. No matter what we face or how tough it gets, we must get this project done. So let the mockery be the fuel for your greatness.

Don't let people mock you and get away with it because the best revenge for mockery is success in the very thing you were mocked for, so you can imagine how the Sheikh of Dubai feels today when he reads all the Western media that mocked him, especially when Dubai had economic crises in 2008 and 2009. Everything had to stop: all construction stopped, Dubai owed 100 billion dollars, and everything stopped in Dubai. Every billionaire has once been called a scammer. Alibaba's Jack Ma, one of my role models in business, was mocked; in fact, I saw one on national television saying, "Jack, people say you're a scammer; you keep raising funds and collecting investor funds, but you guys

"Keep saying it until you see it"

didn't make money." Your company is not raising funds, but young guys aren't making money. On television, I saw them say that to Jack Ma.

Today Jack Ma did the largest IPO ever, and everybody went "Ooh,

Jack Ma, hero of e-commerce", but the reality is that's just the way human beings are wired. They will call you a scammer because you're doing what they're not doing; you've got the guts and the courage, and people will hate your guts if you want to operate in our world. When asked why they don't like Stephen Akintayo, many people say things like, "I just think there's something shady about his confidence, about his guts; he's either a comparatist or a genius; he has to be one of those two."

Somebody said this to me, and I smiled. I really couldn't stop smiling. I said, "Well, anyone you choose to believe is OK, but I'm me." But what I love about this whole thing is that results will permanently terminate insults, so don't take things personally. I've learned not to take criticism personally. You know, people have their opinions and their concerns. You can't blame them. Keep your vision alive. Set your goals. Chase your goals, believe in your goals, talk about your goals, and tell people about your goals even before you even achieve them, whether they believe in your goals or not, whether they believe in your dreams or not; you keep telling them, "I have a dream; one day I'm going to be a billionaire," so keep speaking about it until you see it; the boldness to talk about it is what ultimately creates it. If you're scared to say it, you will never see it. I've seen a lot of scared people! They are too afraid to share their dream; it is your dream, it is your vision, not theirs. So, keep saying it until you see it.

If you think it's been easy for me, then you don't know me. I've had harrowing experiences as I've tried to grow my business, but my secret is that I don't give up. One of the secrets you must have is to say what you want to see, not what you see now. Talk about where you're going and not where you are. Some of us are too busy talking about where we are. If you care about where you are, you want to focus on where you are going. Tell people where you're going. Help people see where you're going even before you get there so that when you get there, they're going to say, "We remember when he kept saying it when he used to say it."

So many people who knew me years ago always talk about how I used to say these things. I used to know him when he was on campus. I used to know him when he just stared at his business; he used to have this big mouth, and he used to say he would be this or that. That guy was very arrogant. But, whether I like him or not, he has done more than what he told us, and that's the secret, guys. A lot of what I said then, I've even done more than those things. A lot of what I was sharing with people about what I was going to do, I've dusted those records.

We've passed the point where we're talking about a scarier version now. The truth is this, and don't ever forget this: in this whole universe, 75% of the people in the world do not know what is happening; they are only victims of what is happening. Another 20% know what is happening but are not part of it; they analyze it. Elon Musk is going to do this; there's this new project happening; they talk about it; they're not participating. Only 5% of the people in the world make things happen, and only 5% are responsible for the changes, actions, and transformations happening in this world. So, where do you want to be?

CHAPTER EIGHT

HABIT 7: KEEP MANUFACTURING

"...we've decided to be the producers, manufacturers, and world changers—the people who shape the world!"

Do you want to be one of the 95% or one of the 5%? Do you want to be a victim or a victor? Do you want to be a consumer or a manufacturer? Do you want to consume analyses that lead to paralysis and talk and talk and talk without being a part of the creative process of changing the world?

So, I'm a world changer and one of the 5% changing my world. So, choose your world; it's up to you, but as for my family and me, we've decided to be the producers, manufacturers, and world changers—the people who shape the world.

Poor people are paid for their time, but billionaires are paid for their value, productivity, and results. Have you ever wondered why billionaires are never paid per hour? Think about billionaires like Elon Musk, Bill Gates, Jeff Bezos, Warren Buffett, Aliko Dangote, Jack Ma, and Oprah Winfrey. Can you imagine how much these people would be paid per hour? the amount will be stupendously ridiculous.

"Poor people are paid for their time, but billionaires are paid for their value, productivity, and results."

That is why no one discusses paying billionaires by the hour. Instead, they are paid based on the value they bring to the marketplace. They are compensated based on the results they have achieved over several years. Most billionaires spend ten years or more building wealth and achieving the results they are paid for. Think about Amazon, Microsoft, Ali Baba, Dangote's companies, and many other billion-dollar brands. How long did it take them to make such a name for themselves? That is a key principle about wealth generation that many poor people don't understand. Building a billion-dollar brand takes a long time. But the good thing

"One of the most powerful contributions you can make to any organization is to focus on results."

about such brands, once they reach world-class status, they are likely to remain there for generations.

People often contact me and say they want to meet with me. But after directing them to schedule a time for such meetings with my secretary, I usually see the disappointment on their faces or notice it in their voice. But the truth is that for me to continue to be effective, I must work according to a schedule. Therefore, I cannot afford to have unplanned meetings with my friends, relatives, and family members, who may take most of my time just talking about things that have no direct bearing on my business or productivity. Therefore, before I meet with you, I must first ascertain the purpose of the planned meeting. How is this meeting going to enhance my productivity? How is our meeting going to be mutually beneficial?

Because most poor people do not understand the principle of focusing on results, when they start a business or join a company, they often assume that they are productive by simply coming to work early and closing late. For those who work for others, the assumption is that mere punctuality is enough to grant them a promotion. In our company, we don't promote people because of their punctuality. We promote them based on their productivity and results. This does not mean that we are not strict on punctuality. We emphasize punctuality but place productivity above it. If you spend five hours in the office, we are more concerned about the results you have produced within those hours than we are about your presence in the office.

One of the most powerful contributions you can make to

any organization is to focus on results. If you can help your organization either make more or save money, you are considered a great asset to the organization. No CEO would want to let go of such staff. This is because when you help your organization save money or make more money, you are building the brand equity of that organization. If you contribute toward making your company grow its brand equity or have a better name, you have earned the right to become a great asset to your company. But in situations where you are punctual in reporting to work without improving the business results, you become a liability to the organization. You are almost on your way out whenever you are not found to be adding tangible value. No responsible manager or supervisor will want to promote such an employee.

CHAPTER NINE

HABIT 8: CONSISTENTLY BUILD HIGH-VALUE NETWORKS

"The quality of your relationships, connections, and network says a lot about the kind of business you are likely to build."

The person who lacks the humility to work for others to gain experience and acquire some capital before starting his business misses out on many advantageous opportunities. Remember, the biggest asset you can ever have is a valuable network and relationship. It is the most effective tool for curbing poverty. The quality of your relationships, connections, and network says a lot about the kind of business you are likely to build. Therefore, never take the opportunity to work with experienced people and learn from them for granted. There are just certain things that money cannot buy, and one of them is the experience that comes from valuable people, networks, associations, and organizations. Relationships become significant assets when you are just starting. Remember that having a great product is not enough; you have to leverage other people's networks and connections to market your product.

Most billionaires started working for existing companies already doing what they anticipated creating. They gained experience, understood the system, and sharpened their ideas through that process. That is most common in the technology and software sectors. Brian Acton and Jan Koum, who created WhatsApp, for instance, had worked for Yahoo! before leaving to start their company. Such is the story of many billionaires. They first set out to work for companies that are doing the same thing they plan to do—gaining experience in the field—before leaving to start their own companies. That way, they have a significant advantage when they start because they can avoid making unnecessary mistakes that could cost them so much.

Most billionaires started their businesses by referring people to other companies. Almost all billionaires sacrificed some time serving others and gaining experience before launching their businesses. But most people lack the patience to serve and learn from others. When they have an idea, they want to rush into it without having the patience to work with people who are already doing similar things to gain some experience. For example, Aliko Dangote started his business by referring people to his uncle's trading business. Chief Razaq Akanni Okoya, the famed Nigerian billionaire industrialist, also had a humble start. He started by working for his father in the tailoring business, including selling tailoring accessories. Through that, he was able to save some money before he later started his importation business.

For instance, before Mark Zuckerberg, the Founder and CEO of Facebook, purchased Instagram and WhatsApp from their owners to become part of his social networking businesses, he had already spent several years as one of the early pioneers in that technological field to know the kind of social networks that were going to be successful and add more value to his already successful businesses. Also, before the owners of Google purchased YouTube, they had done much feasibility research and understood the value that such a video-sharing site would add to their company.

I can give several examples of the different companies that Jeff Bezos has purchased to become part of Amazon over the years. That has become the trend and culture among billionaires, especially the Founders and CEOs of the Great Four: Facebook, Apple, Amazon, and Google.

Billionaires understand that to be successful, you must take full responsibility for your actions and stop blaming others for your misfortunes. People who always play the "victim mentality" do not make meaningful progress in life.

"Billionaires understand that to be successful, you must take full

responsibility for your actions and stop blaming others for your misfortunes."

Jack Canfield, the author of the best-selling book, The Success Principles, put it better: "If you want to be successful, you have to take 100% responsibility for everything that you experience in your life." "This includes the level of your achievements, the results you produce, the quality of your relationships, the state of your health and physical fitness, your income, your debts, your feelings—everything!"

Billionaires have studied and mastered the art of scaling so much that when they do, people rush in to put their money there because they are confident that they are putting their money in something that has been demonstrated to be worthwhile over time. As a result, even if such businesses fail to generate the expected profit, investors do not become unduly harsh on themselves for being foolish, nor do they blame the business owners for deceiving them. They would think that maybe something went wrong, and that was why the business model failed. That is what they will try to find out. They try not to take the business owner to court unless there is clear evidence of recklessness and mismanagement of resources.

But for many poor people, the moment they have a business idea, they want to ask other people to give them a loan or invest in their idea. While there are confident investors that may want to take a chance on such initiatives, most investors only invest in businesses that have proven workable over time and have a standard operational principle. If you make the mistake of collecting people's money before starting your business, and you are unlucky, and the business fails, you ruin your

"Remember, investors care about track records."

reputation and many will find it difficult to trust you in the future, even if you bring up something legitimate. People may call you names, and some may even take legal action against you by labelling you a thief, scammer, or the like. Remember, investors, care about track records.

Earlier, I decided that I would not start raising capital for my real estate company until after we had successfully run the business for some time and built a name and credibility for ourselves. Having demonstrated credibility and shown the world that we know what we are doing, we can scale and ask others to invest in our company. I can confidently say that we have already achieved that status. We have demonstrated that we know how to acquire land in the right location. Since we have already built a structure and a brand and have become a multi-billion naira real estate company in Africa, if we decide to scale today and ask people to invest in our company, do you think anyone is going to be suspicious of our operations or doubt our credibility?

Most billionaires started by working for existing companies that were already doing what they anticipated creating. Through that process, they gained experience, understood the system, and sharpened their ideas. This is mostly common in the technology and software sectors. Brain Acton and Jack Koum, who created WhatsApp, for instance, had worked for Yahoo! before leaving to start their company. Such is the story with many billionaires. They first set out to work for companies that are doing the same thing that they plan to do—gaining experience in the field—before leaving to start their own companies. That way, they have a great advantage when they start in that they can avoid making unnecessary mistakes that could cost them so much.

The person who lacks the humility to work for others to gain experience and acquire some capital before starting his business misses out on a lot of advantageous opportunities.

Remember, the biggest asset you can ever have is a valuable network and relationship.

"The person who lacks the humility to work for others to gain experience and acquire some capital before starting his business

misses out on many advantageous opportunities."

It is the most effective tool for curbing poverty. The quality of your relationships, connections, and network says a lot about the kind of business you are likely to build. Therefore, never take the opportunity to work with experienced people and learn from them for granted. There are just certain things that money cannot buy, and one of them is the experience that comes from valuable people, networks, associations, and organizations. Relationships become significant assets when you are just starting. Remember that having a great product is not enough; you have to leverage other people's networks and connections to market your product.

Here is a practical example of something that has come to characterize my business dealings. Because I have employed skilled and capable people to handle the various operations of my companies, sometimes I travel to our offices in Dubai, the United States, or the United Kingdom and stay outside Nigeria for three months or more while my businesses in Nigeria continue to run smoothly and thrive. The same thing applies when I leave those countries where we have businesses. Many people in those offices handle the daily operations of my businesses in our various offices outside Nigeria, so even if I decide to stay in Nigeria for several months without visiting those offices, I can sleep well because I trust my employees and partners. As I write this, I have spent my last three months outside Nigeria, but my staff have opened and launched new estates in Nigeria. How did they manage to do that without my presence? Because I have trained them to be acquainted with the company's various operations of the company that I don't have to be there before something significant takes place. So, while I am busy expanding our businesses in Dubai and elsewhere, my staff in Nigeria are busy opening and launching several estates in my absence. That is what the art of scaling looks like.

If you plan to build a lasting business that will scale, you must be willing to put a structure in place and employ other people's time so the business can run smoothly and thrive without your constant involvement and monitoring. Because of the lack of such structures, most poor people who start businesses get easily upset and frustrated and assume that they are not lucky.

BILLIONAIRES AND VISIONARY RELATIONSHIPS

Billionaires are visionary people. Let me reiterate that when I talk about billionaires, I am not referring to corrupt politicians who have stolen people's money or become billionaires without working diligently for what they have. This clarification is necessary because, in Africa, many people become rich in the sweat of others due to rampant cases of corruption. Those are not the kinds of people I am talking about. And because of this unfortunate situation of rampant corruption, the average African perceives every rich person as corrupt. Billionaires are visionary. What is a vision? It is the ability to see beyond the ordinary. In other words, a vision involves projecting future goals and a conscientious determination to achieve them. I particularly like how Bill Hybels defines vision; he says, "Vision is the picture of the future that produces passion." It is visionary people who change the world. A visionary is someone who can see beyond his present circumstances and be excited and passionate about the future. Billionaires are visionary people, and it is not surprising that their circle of influence tends to comprise people who are changing the world differently.

THE BILLIONAIRES CIRCLE

In my entire life, I am yet to meet a billionaire who is a gossip. Billionaires only associate, relate and interact with people who have a vision. That is why it is difficult for billionaires to waste time gossiping, whining, or castigating others. They don't have time for that. When they meet with others, they have something important that they want to discuss that will benefit them. They always think about their future goals and do not hesitate to seize every opportunity to discuss their visions and goals. Since gossip always has to do with what is wrong or bad about another person, it follows that people who waste their time gossiping about others are visionless. If you don't have a specific vision in life, you wouldn't mind talking about others who do. One of the ironies of life is that visionaries create goals and accomplish incredible feats that visionless people revel in talking about, either favourably or unfavourably. In the end, visionaries do not care what you think about what they achieve.

"Visionaries create goals and accomplish great feats that visionless people revel in talking about, either favourably or unfavourably."

They are so preoccupied with many goals that they don't have time to waste listening to or reading comments or gossip about who likes or hates them. When they achieve one goal, they quickly move to the next big thing. Let me share with you one of the secrets of rich and famous people: They dominate social media with their content and have a large following on those platforms, not necessarily because they spend so much time there. They create content for poor and visionless people who spend hours upon hours consuming them. The moment a rich person posts something on social media, he leaves and finds something essential to do. Most of them do not have time to read people's comments on their posts because doing so will detract them from their vision. In other words, visionaries create content for visionless people to spend many hours consuming while the visionaries make money.

CHAPTER TEN

HABIT 9: MAKING MONEY

"One of the major secrets to building wealth is service."

1. Service Provision

One of the major secrets to building wealth is service. Service is the pathway to greatness. Every billionaire started by offering service to people. Unfortunately, the concept of service has been given a bad name in contemporary times. Many people want to be bosses and have lots of money, but they are unwilling to do what it takes to reach that status. They seem unwilling to serve.

"Every billionaire started by offering service to people."

Referral marketing is a way of providing a twofold service to people. First, you serve the company by expanding its business through sales and popularity. Second, you serve people who need those products by connecting them with the appropriate companies. No wonder such services bring many returns.

Let me share the secret of how I started my real estate business. I did not start with money. My parents were not wealthy, so I did not inherit any money from them to give me a good and easy start. I knew that I wanted to go into encumbrance. As such, I decided that I would not allow my lack of startup capital to stop me. You may be wondering, "How then did I succeed in building a multi-billion naira real estate empire without having a startup capital?" It was through referral services. I decided that I would find some existing real estate companies and make a deal with them to provide them with referral marketing services. That was exactly what happened. Since I and those companies had mutual trust, it was not long before I started referring people to them. They kept to their promise and started paying me 10 percent of every sale they made through my referral services. They had many customers through my referral services, and I earned money in return for

"Billionaires provide service before making products!"

Those services. It was a win-win situation for everyone. When I sold ten million naira worth of land, for example, I earned one million naira. Sometimes, I got lucky and sold a property worth fifty million naira and earned five million naira from it. I kept saving my earnings because I had a vision. Eventually, I saved enough to start my own real estate company.

The point is worth repeating that most billionaires start their businesses without capital. But instead of rushing to start, they take their time to work for others who are providing similar services that they anticipate providing in their company. One of the easiest ways to establish business relationships with companies is through referral marketing, which allows one to pursue other goals. Since referrals are based on sales percentages, the business model is quite flexible.

Billionaires provide service before making products. Cosmos Maduka, the Nigerian businessman and Founder of Coscharis Group, began his career working for his uncle in the automobile industry before being wrongfully fired and deciding to start his own company. Most billionaires have similar stories. But unless one cares to find out how they started, there is always the wrong assumption that they started big. What billionaires have learned to do better than the rest is prioritize services over products.

Because most people are always thinking about and motivated by money, they start a business with a product without taking time to think about the kind of service they are well-positioned to offer to the public. They fail to recognize that selling a product is far more complex than providing a service. Services give you a good understanding of business principles. And it is easier to become known by providing services than by selling products. That is a significant characteristic of consumer behaviour. Providing service helps you understand customer behaviour and needs.

"Volume is what makes businesses scale and become billion dollar companies."

That is why it is crucial to start your business as a service before moving to a product. Microsoft, Ali Baba, Amazon, Apple, Google, Virgin, PayPal, and many other multi-Billion dollar companies did not start as products but as services. They noticed a societal problem and set out to solve it by providing a service. A service does not need a product but can transition into one. Anyone who can provide a service efficiently and effectively can raise capital to start developing products. You can hardly find a billionaire who started by launching a product. They all started with service before they later developed products.

2. Business Volume

Billionaires always start with services before moving on to products. But the mere transition to products is not enough to make a business succeed. Therefore, they use the principle of volume to scale their businesses. The quantity of products circulated at any given time is referred to as "business volume." More specifically, it deals with the number of products that a company produces, sells, and makes profits

"The quantity of products circulated at any given time is referred to as "business volume."

at any given time. The demand for volume can come from personal or group needs.

Volume is what makes businesses scale and become billion-dollar companies. Amazon, for instance, is a trillion-dollar company because of its volume. With close to a million employees, Amazon leverages volume to outdo every online business company in the world through the products and services it provides to people in many parts of the world, as they do not randomly create a product in a million quantities and start selling. The strategy they use is first to test the

"In business, numbers speak louder than any other factor."

Product in the market to ascertain whether it is going to fly. The saying goes, "Nothing can happen until someone sells something." To know whether your product is ready for volume, it must first pass the tests of validation and consumption. The test of validation relates to the number of people talking about the product's uniqueness. The test of consumption has to do with the number of people who have bought the product and found it helpful. In the world of business, numbers speak louder than any other factor. The tests of validation and consumption reveal your numbers and help you decide whether you are ready for volume.

Business volume rests on two key factors: demand and supply. The law of demand states that "quantity purchased varies inversely with price." In other words, the higher the price of a product, the lower the quantity demanded.

Conversely, the lower the product price, the higher the demand. If you want to maximize volume in your business, you must pay attention to the law of demand, that is, how expensive your product is compared to other products in the market. You must learn to pay attention to the need for the product and its affordability in the market.

On the other hand, the supply law states, "All other factors being equal, as the price of a good or service increases, the number of goods or services that suppliers offer will increase, and vice versa." In other words, the higher the price of a product, the more the suppliers will want to increase the volume of the product to maximize profit.

Both the law of demand and the law of supply are essential

variables to pay attention to before you increase your business volume. If you ignore these

"Speed is only useful if you're running in the right direction."

key factors and go about increasing your business volume based on instincts or assumptions, you are likely to accrue losses if it turns out that your assumptions were wrong. That is why it is essential to pay attention to demand and supply before applying the volume principle in your business. Joel Barker says, "Speed is only useful if you're running in the right direction." Therefore, never make assumptions about the quality and demand of your product and use that assumption to increase its volume. Have the patience to study the facts, for facts never lie.

"Understanding the laws of demand and supply will help you make informed and more accurate decisions about volume."

Higher market demand for a product is always a good indicator that the product is ready to scale using volume. That is why understanding the laws of demand, and supply help you make informed and more accurate decisions about volume.

Here is a practical example that buttresses this point. I do a lot of paid coaching for people. One of my students in my coaching program wanted to scale his transportation business and needed my help. He told me he wanted to transform his transportation business into a particular product. He got the product cheaply and had an exclusive deal with the manufacturer. He had set aside fifty million naira for the product, but he wanted to share it with me before signing the deal. After listening to him and asking him key questions, I thought the decision was not smart given the volume he wanted to start the business with. So I advised him to the contrary. I told him, "I would advise you to hold on with the volume. It doesn't mean that putting that huge amount into "the product" may not bring great returns, but you need to test-run the product first in the market with a small amount. That will allow you to make more informed decisions based on the realities of demand and supply." I specifically advised him to start with one million naira rather than put fifty million naira into something he was unsure about. I probably would have told him to start with a One hundred thousand naira or less, had he not told me about the fifty million he was willing to put into the business.

Because billionaires often start with referrals, they start with good capital that enables them to scale faster and increase the volume of their business much sooner than others who start small. But remember that they first have to sacrifice by working for others and gaining capital to start well. Many poor people start small that they never have people who will guide, coach, or mentor them in business.

Most importantly, they do not start as a service. They are always thinking about products, not services. And even when they want to start with products, they always seem to be in such a hurry that they hardly take time to do feasibility studies to consider such variables as demand and supply. So at the end, they don't have enough capital to scale, and they fail to have volume because they never have time to test the idea in the market.

3. Business Acquisition

Billionaires prefer to make money by acquiring structurally thriving businesses rather than building new ones. This preference is because most billionaires have built businesses from the ground up and know how rigorous and challenging starting new businesses can be. Billionaires prefer to acquire thriving enterprises rather than start them all over again.

"Billionaires prefer to make money by acquiring structurally thriving businesses rather than building new ones."

People who start new businesses and are willing to sell them stand to benefit from billionaires who are looking for new businesses to acquire or invest in. But billionaires do not acquire any new business just because it is new. The owners of the business must have proven their worth and scaled the business to a reasonable extent before they can attract billionaires' interest. Hundreds of thousands of new businesses never attract the attention of billionaires simply because the owners have not brought something unique to the marketplace to attract billionaire investors or acquirers. Sometimes the business idea may be good, but billionaires are not looking for just good business ideas. They are looking for good business ideas that can scale and bring them significant profits upon their acquisition. Remember that billionaires have spent so much time on the business trail that they know which can easily scale and profit and which cannot.

"Hundreds of thousands of new businesses never attract the attention of billionaires simply because the owners have not brought something unique to the marketplace to attract billionaire investors or acquirers."

For instance, before Mark Zuckerberg, the Founder and CEO of Facebook, purchased Instagram and WhatsApp from their owners to become part of his social networking businesses, he had already spent several years as a pioneer in that technological field, determining the types of social networks that would be successful and add value to his already successful businesses. Also, before the owners of Google purchased YouTube, they had done much feasibility research and understood the value that such a video-sharing site would add to their company. I can give several examples of the different companies that Jeff Bezos has purchased to become part of Amazon over the years. That has become the trend and culture among billionaires, especially the founders and CEOs of the Great Four: Facebook, Apple, Amazon, and Google.

That is a practical example of what I plan to do in our company in the coming years. I want to start expanding our business in the technology sector. That is to say; our company will begin looking for great startups in the technology sectors, particularly applications and software developed by Africans, to acquire.

"Many talented young people in Africa have great ideas."

The reason is twofold. First, I realized that westerners have taken over a lot of the tech businesses that started in Africa. It beats my imagination that African billionaires are not investing in our tech businesses. Second, at this point in my life, I do not want to start new companies from scratch; I would instead acquire the ones that have already been developed and proven to scale.

Paystack, a Nigerian startup company that processes payment problems for businesses in Africa, was acquired for 200 million dollars by Stripe, owned by non-Africans. The question is, aren't there Nigerian or African billionaires that would have acquired Paystack? African politicians and rich people prefer to invest in foreign companies than in African startups to encourage innovation and entrepreneurship. That has got to stop. While Nigerians love to complain that foreigners have taken over all their businesses, it seems like most Africans prefer foreign things than what they have. Many talented young people in Africa have great ideas. For Africa to thrive and meet the challenges of the twenty-first century, there must be a change of mentality about business, innovation, and entrepreneurship.

When billionaires reach a certain level of wealth, they stop thinking about starting new businesses and instead focus on acquiring existing ones. It does not matter whether a company's owners have shown interest in selling or not. When billionaires see a business with good prospects, they approach the owners and make them an offer for its acquisition. And most of these offers can be pretty enticing and challenging to resist. While some owners may refuse a billionaire's acquisition offer, such as Snapchat's refusal to accept Mark

"At this point in my career, I would rather acquire an existing business than start a new one."

Zuckerberg's $3 Billion acquisition offer, many find the

temptation too strong to resist.

How did Bill Gates become the owner of more than one hundred different companies besides Microsoft? He certainly did not start all of them. He acquired existing businesses or became one of the major stakeholders in the businesses. After spending decades building Microsoft from the ground up to become a world-class company, he could not afford to start the same process all over again to build different companies. He, therefore, leveraged his billionaire status and acquired several other businesses without having to sweat for them.

Billionaires understand how difficult and time-consuming it is to start a business. And because they are not willing to tread on the same path they are familiar with, they prefer to acquire other businesses. Anyone who has ever started a business would confirm that such an enterprise requires resilience, consistency, and agility. Hence, many wouldn't want to repeat the process even if they successfully did it the first time.

At this point in my career, I would instead acquire an existing business than start a new one.

The acquisition is much simpler to do. All it takes is to look out for a good business that seems to be struggling to scale, make the owners an offer, acquire it if they are willing to accept my offer, and then use my experience and resources to scale it. If I decide to own a radio or television station, I do not have time to start such a process from scratch. Instead, I would acquire an existing radio or television station and use my resources to scale it. That is how billionaires think.

Business acquisition is one of the powerful secrets of billionaires. Most billionaires have mastered three skills: **how to make money, manage money, and multiply money.** Then, they apply these skills to acquire other businesses.

Instead of acquiring new businesses, some billionaires may

become angel investors. An angel investor has economic solid capital and is willing to invest in new businesses in exchange for equity in the business or some convertible debt. Such a person is willing to risk putting his capital into a great business idea with the hope that it will scale and bring profits.

Billionaires who decide to become angel investors are risk-takers. Because of the risk involved in such investments, angel investors are always looking for a higher percentage of profit and returns. They typically ask for percentages of return as high as twenty-five to sixty per cent. That is because the business has "already scaled." That explains why many billionaires refrain from investing as angels. But even the few that defy the odds and do it go into the process with much caution. They take their time to do much research about the business idea and the owners before putting their money into it. They always want to be sure that the risk they are about to take is worth the pain.

4. Venture Capitalists

A venture capitalist invests a substantial amount of money in a business that has already accrued a significant amount of revenue. In other words, venture capitalists invest in businesses that have already scaled. Such investments are usually in the millions of dollars. Venture capitalists get their returns through hedge funds or private equity, whereby they receive a certain percentage of the profits that the companies they have invested in making.

One of the advantages of the venture capitalist business model is that it helps businesses scale and provide volume. In doing so, also establishes credibility for the company. That way, both the company and the investors gain from the partnership. While the company's owners rejoice because of the company's expansion and volume, the venture capitalists also have reasons to rejoice because of the percentage of profit they gain from their investment in the company. That is one simple but clever way for billionaires to multiply their wealth.

5. Passive Income

Billionaires create systems that continuously generate money without constant monitoring or active involvement in the process.

Such income is what is technically known as passive income. Specifically, passive income is the money earned automatically with little or no effort on the part of the earner.

The nomenclature "passive" can be misleading. Many people hear the word "passive income" and immediately think of someone earning money that they do not deserve. They think of using magic formulas like affirmations and voodoo to generate continuous income that they have not worked for. But in reality, passive income is not passive. It demands action on the part of the earner, at least at the beginning, when one works hard to set up such a reliable system of money generation. It only becomes passive after one has laboriously

"If you don't find a way to make money while you sleep, you will work until you die." - Warren Buffet.

Put in place a working system that continues to generate income constantly and automatically. A few examples of passive income ideas will help explain the concept.

It is not news that many billionaires make much money from real estate. In other words, they purchase properties and rent them out, eventually becoming their major passive income source. Rental activities are a sure way to create passive income. Most landlords receive a monthly income from their rental property consistently without having to interact with their tenants or do anything specifically. Because they have already purchased the property and put a system in place that continues to generate money for them, they are confident of receiving a certain amount of money on a monthly or annual basis from their tenants. They usually do not need to do anything other than this.

The same thing goes for authors. Writing a book can be a time-consuming and exhausting endeavour. But when a book is published and begins to generate income, there is no limit to how much income the author will continue to get from the sales of the book. Book sales income can outlive the author and, in some cases, last for centuries, depending on the success and relevance of the book. One successful book is enough to change a person's financial future. In this sense, a successfully published book can be a source of passive income for the author.

Warren Buffet has two poignant statements on the concept of passive income. On one occasion, he was quoted , "You can never be rich until you make money while you sleep." On another occasion, Buffett said, "If you don't find a way to make money while you sleep, you will work until you die." The two statements are closely related. On the one hand, Buffett demonstrates the importance of developing a system that generates money while requiring little or no effort. But, on the other hand, he points to the danger of endless toiling for income, which is characteristic of billions of people worldwide.

People who believe that working constantly is the only way to make money are more likely to die working. Such people work with the erroneous mentality that money is earned through daily toil. They fail to realize that such a work mentality does not make people rich. People who build wealth have put specific systems in place that continue to generate money for them while they are asleep. That is one of the major secrets of billionaires.

"People who believe that working constantly is the only way to make money are more likely to die working."

Billionaires make money while they sleep. After building a proven system of wealth generation and cash flow, they go to sleep while they continue to enjoy great returns from that system. These systems range from real estate to different kinds of investments and businesses. At the beginning of their careers, however, they worked hard almost daily for several years until they have a solid financial base and built a system for generating passive income. After that, they begin to leverage their hard work by creating many more passive income generation systems while finding time to rest, have fun, and enjoy the benefits of their investments.

To create a system that generates passive income, you must apply wisdom to your work from day one. Remember, passive income does not just happen; it is created. It is wisdom when you concentrate your energy and attention on building specific structures and systems that will generate money for you while you sleep. For instance, you can create online courses or videos, write a book, run a blog, start a drop-shipping store, create an app, invest in stocks, do affiliate marketing, and explore several other creative ideas. It is all about applying wisdom from where you are to get what you want.

"You can never be financially independent until you are able to put a system in place that generates money for you while you sleep!"

Billionaires are always thinking outside the box. They are primarily unconventional in the way they approach business. That is one of the qualities of having "secured" jobs, which give them the guarantee of such things as retirement benefits, a monthly salary, job security, and health insurance. They abhor going against anything that appears to be unconventional. As such, the idea of passive income often seems strange to them. Such people do not know how to automate. They are always working hard but not brilliant. It is as if they have willfully surrendered their will to the control of another person or organization. They fail to realize that, through the application of wisdom, they can create systems that work best for them and bring them guaranteed income while they sleep and enjoy what they have.

Conventional jobs mean that one may continue to work until retirement without having time to enjoy the fruits of his labour. At best, he realizes that all his work is geared toward paying bills. But not so with people who have a billionaire mindset. For such people, rather than work to pay bills, they put little or no effort into it and continue to be paid for the services that their systems provide to others. With little or no effort, they keep becoming richer through the systems they have set up.

You can never be financially independent until you can put a system in place that generates money for you while you sleep. The way to know that you have attained the status of financial freedom and independence is to scrutinize

"Real estate is one of the major secrets of billionaires' passive income."

your income-generating systems. What makes you money? How often do you receive such an income? Can anything happen overnight that will threaten the flow of that income? Do you have to work hard to earn that income? Can you go on a vacation anytime you want without feeling guilty about skipping work? Do other people pay you anonymously?

Real estate is one of the major secrets of billionaires' passive income. It is difficult to find a billionaire who does not own real estate that generates passive income. It is the easiest way toward financial freedom.

I am sharing this because a lady came to our office a couple of days ago and was smiling. When I tried to inquire about what was making her so enthusiastic, she reported that she had just sold the property she bought from us three years earlier and gained six million naira in profit from it. She bought the property from us at the cost of Two million naira. Can you imagine gaining such a profit in such a short time? Some time later, she told me that she had specifically come to the office to show appreciation for our company. That is how people become billionaires. Wise people create a system and build a structure that guarantees the flow of income into their bank accounts without having to worry about most of life's contingencies that millions of people think about and worry about.

CHAPTER ELEVEN

HABIT 10: MULTIPLICATION MINDSET

"Embrace the principle of replication!"

No business can grow exponentially without applying certain principles. Billionaires enjoy making money, but they derive more pleasure from multiplying their wealth and businesses. The idea of multiplication suggests that one has already made money and needs to go to the next level to increase it. For example, how does one turn a ten million dollar enterprise into a hundred million dollar business? How can one grow and expand a hundred million dollar company into a billion dollar company?

"Billionaires enjoy making money, but they derive more pleasure from multiplying their wealth and businesses."

If you are not yet a millionaire, you need to learn how to become one before learning how to become a billionaire. These principles are relevant because once you become a millionaire, you want to know how to multiply your money to the next level and possibly become a billionaire.

1. The principle of replication

When billionaires are ready to multiply their wealth, they follow the principle of replication. In business, the replication principle deals with the conscious repetition of a validated success to continue generating growth and expansion. Billionaires apply the replication principle in two significant ways.

They begin by multiplying themselves among others. They make it a point to intentionally mentor others by sharing their wealth of experience. Through many years of experience —years of successes and failures, pains and gains, excitements and disappointments—they have understood and applied life principles that are not taught in formal academic settings. Knowing this, they intentionally mentor and coach other people of like minds to follow and apply these principles for maximum success in life.

Secondly, they replicate their businesses. Billionaires not only seek to replicate their life principles to help others succeed but also try to replicate their business models in different ventures for maximum growth and expansion. By applying the same work principles in different business settings, they keep sharpening and strengthening those principles to make them relevant and applicable in any business setting.

A principle, by definition, is a proven way of life that can be applied under any given circumstance to produce desired results. Ray Dalio, an American billionaire businessman, hedge fund manager, Founder of Bridgewater Associates, and author of the bestselling book Principles, emphasizes that "principles are fundamental truths that serve as the foundation for behaviour that gets you what you want out of life."

They can be applied again and again in similar situations to help you achieve your goals. He further explains that "all successful people operate by principles that help them be successful, though what they choose to be successful at varies enormously, so their principles vary."

"Anyone who fails to intentionally replicate himself in another person's life is most likely to be soon forgotten."

One of the major regrets that rich, famous, and influential people often have toward the end of their lives is the failure to replicate themselves in other people. No matter how vast the wealth or businesses you have acquired or built are, someday you will be no more. And when you are gone, other people will take charge of everything you have worked hard to accumulate. When that happens, your heirs may either expand or demolish those businesses. To avoid a scenario whereby everything you have worked hard to achieve automatically dissipates shortly after you are gone, you must be conscious and determined to replicate yourself in the lives of other people you would want to take after you. These may be your family members (spouse, children, siblings, or distant relatives), trusted business colleagues, or anyone you are interested in grooming. Anyone who fails to intentionally replicate himself in another person's life is most likely to be soon forgotten.

I've grown to trust a Nigerian lady who has lived in Dubai over the years. Because I have been mentoring her for quite some time now and have tried to replicate myself in her, it was easy for me to assign her the herculean responsibility of running our Gtext Dubai office. Despite that, after opening the office, I still had to stay in Dubai for a month to coach her about certain principles of running a business like ours. I want her to be able to think about business the way I do so she can contribute immensely to Gtext's effectiveness and growth in Dubai. Through intentional mentoring and coaching, our new administrative staff in Dubai will be able to replicate my life and work principles even in my absence. When I leave, I don't have to stress about the daily running of our Dubai office because I know that I have put someone in charge who can operate the business the way I would. The same principle applies to our Abuja, United States, and United Kingdom offices. Some people must run those offices.

"To scale your business, you must teach others your life and business principles."

The most important thing I need to do is make sure I have replicated myself in those people so they can have the same life and work principles as me. But this cannot happen by chance. It must involve a conscious effort on my part to train and mentor others to think and approach business the way I do.

Unfortunately, most people are often hesitant to share the secrets of their lives and businesses with others. They prefer to hide from others the principles they use to achieve success. Such people wrongly assume that teaching, mentoring, and coaching others to use the same systems they use will result in those people overtaking them. Therefore, they hide those systems and principles from others so that no one can replicate what they do. When they find a particular life or business principle to be beneficial, they do everything possible to hide it from others.

To live and die well, you must learn to replicate yourself in others, except if that which you want to replicate will not benefit them.

That is an important distinction because so many people often prefer to replicate their negative experiences in the lives of others. If they try something and fail, they also want others to go through the same thing and experience the pain they have experienced. Such replication efforts are, at best, detrimental and ill-conceived.

If you do not allow anyone to know what your success secrets are, you are stunting your growth and the potential of grooming other people who will replicate your principles for the betterment of society. That is why many people never scale their businesses. To scale your business, you must teach others your life and business principles. There is a dimension of what you know and who you are that you must pour into other people. If you are sure that other people will represent you well and do what you are doing to succeed in life and business, then there is no reason for you to refuse to share. Under such circumstances, refusing to share may be considered selfishness. One of the people I respect the most in this area is Tony Elumelu, the Nigerian economist, entrepreneur, philanthropist, and founder of the Tony Elumelu Foundation. His foundation was established "based on the belief that, with the right support, entrepreneurs can be empowered to contribute meaningfully to Africa's prosperity and social development." One of Elumelu's powerful secrets is his ability to replicate himself in people. As such, he does not struggle to have good, competent, and outstanding people working for him. That is a skill anyone who desires to multiply his business must endeavour to have.

With the way Elumelu has been a trailblazer in the area of entrepreneurship and philanthropy in Africa, I believe that in no distant time, he is most likely to become the wealthiest man in Africa. The reason for such a projection is not implausible: Elumelu has an unequalled ability to replicate leaders—and great leaders, for that matter. He is conscious and determined about how he goes about mentoring, coaching, teaching, and replicating his kind all over Africa. The Tony Elumelu Foundation gives grants to people all over Africa, which has been applauded by many renowned Africans and people worldwide. There is no doubt that Elumelu knows how to look for great leaders, employ them, engage them, and get them to work toward a particular course.

If you must replicate your money, that is, if you plan to multiply your income, you must imbibe the principle of replication. It is one of the secrets that Billionaires use to increase their wealth and influence. They first replicate themselves in other people before they replicate their business principles.

In 2021, we replicated Gtext Homes in Dubai, the United States, and the United Kingdom. My ability as a billionaire to replicate my life and business principles in other people—to open them up to the level of what I know, what I think, and how I think—is essential for the success of our Gtext companies in those various locations. If I do not become vulnerable to them to that extent, it will be difficult for them to run the businesses in those locations successfully. Consequently, I will not be able to keep replicating and enjoying that level of success personally.

A billionaire has the responsibility to replicate not only himself in other people but also the model of the business. You replicate yourself in other people so they can act, think, behave, and approach life and business like you. That is one of the critical characteristics of Billionaires who have been able to build successful businesses.

Have you ever wondered why Apple has continued to thrive after the death of Steve Jobs? It is because Jobs was able to replicate himself in Tim Cook. Jobs replicated his business philosophy and Apple culture in Cook to the extent that there is no glaring difference between their leadership patterns. That is why Apple has continued to be successful. It operates with proven principles that were established and taught by Jobs, its visionary leader.

2. The power of long term investment

In 1997, Jeff Bezos sent his first letter to his company's shareholders. The letter's title was "It is all about the long term." In that letter, the visionary CEO of Amazon, barely three years old, encouraged the shareholders and all his staff to cultivate long term thinking. He told them, "We can't realize our potential as people or companies unless we plan for the long term." Today, I am sure that when those shareholders remember the full content of that communication, they cannot help but be grateful that they trusted Bezos' vision and that it was worth it. As a result, Amazon is today the most extensive online retail company in the world, and Bezos is the world's richest man because he has always considered business a long term investment. Such is the power of vision.

Billionaires think about business and investment based on long term vision and goals. They multiply their money by making long term investments. This way, they can scale their businesses in the long run. They recognize that through patience and perseverance, long term investments usually turn out to build massive wealth.

Elon Musk thought about the long term. He thought of building an electric car even without having any experience working in the automobile industry. But in less than twenty years, he actualized his vision through Tesla, the company he founded. Such a vision sounded outrageous and outlandish at the time, but it has become a reality.

At the time Musk started Tesla or at least said he would start a company that would build electric cars, it didn't make sense to people. He wasn't in the automobile industry when he made that ambitious proclamation, and no one saw the possibility of such an ambitious goal before 2020. But Musk did not only envisage this happening; he also believed it was going to happen, and he was the one who would make it happen. He succeeded because he thought long term and decided to invest for the long haul. He knew it would take a long time to have such a car, but he was ready to pay the price, and today the rest is history. Musk accomplished what he set out to do by setting a long term goal. He could visualize the world he wanted to create and was disciplined enough to follow it through and bring it to fruition.

"Many people are afraid to think big—to see a vision of a great and fabulous future."

Today, Tesla is the only car company in the world that produces cars on a prepaid basis. If you go to the Tesla showroom, you will most likely not see a ready-made car available for purchase. When you want to buy their car, you must preorder it within a couple of months or years before it can be produced.

Billionaires do what their peers do not do today to afford what their peers cannot afford tomorrow. Many people are afraid to think big—to see a vision of a fabulous future. The problem is not so much that people are not ambitious or do not have grand visions for the future. Most people assume that they may not be successful if they share their ambitious future goals with their friends and family members. As a result, they remain silent or abandon such goals entirely.

To think long term, you must learn to think big. David J. Schwartz, the American professor and author of the bestselling book, *The Magic of Thinking Big*, explains, *"Those who believe they can't cannot. "Belief triggers the power to do."* Schwartz said, "Belief in great results is the driving force, the power behind great books, plays, and scientific discoveries." Likewise, belief in success is behind every successful business, church, and political organization. "Belief in success is the basic, essential ingredient of successful people."

Big thinkers consider the long term. Because they have a grand vision of the future, they are patient enough to endure whatever pain the present moment may bring to attain their long term goals. They do not allow today's tribulations and predicaments to distort their vision of the future. Instead, they think about the future they want and go ahead and create it. In other words, they invest in their long term vision.

They make the mistake of saying they want to invest only in thriving businesses and bringing in lots of profits. Because they seek immediate profits, they fail to think about and plan for the future. They only consider the immediate future. But billionaires think twenty, fifty, or even a hundred years ahead.

Gtext is currently the most prominent green and smart home developer in Africa. We aim to become the world's most significant green and smart home developer by 2035 when we hope to have completed 25,000 housing units. But someone may consider my vision too grandiose and idealistic. Some may even think of it as too ambitious. They may say, *"You know you are currently doing well in the business arena." "Why don't you just relax and take things easy?"* We have already started developing Vision 2050 to be the largest organic integrated farm in Africa. Since we know that one of the biggest causes of poverty in Africa is the inability to refine and process natural resources into consumables, we are already thinking and planning toward taking this challenge head-on.

Billionaires do not only consider the present; they also consider the future. Anytime I think business, I think long term. For example, people might take me to undeveloped land in a community.

The land's topography may not show signs of future business prospects or dividends. But since I am always thinking long term, I would show interest in purchasing the land, much to the amazement of many who only think about the here and now. My interest in purchasing the property may not make logical sense to such people. When we first bought the land for our first estate, which later became Sapphire Estate, we could not take customers there to show them the property because it was waterlogged. We could only stand at a distance and point the

"If you don't think long term, it will be increasingly difficult for you to be wealthy."

Land toward them. That constituted a considerable challenge for us. But I was never discouraged. Today, the story is different. The estate is now a beautiful sight to behold because of the amount of work that has gone into it over the years.

Such is the secret of wealth creation. Always think and plan long term because that is what billionaires do. If you don't think long term, it will be increasingly difficult to be wealthy. Most Africans are struggling because everyone is always thinking about short term goals. That is why many Africans would instead join politics to get rich quickly through corrupt practices than think long term and create lasting wealth for their posterity. The idea of a shortcut appeals to many. They hardly realize that shortcuts often end up lengthening the journey more than proper planning and patience would. Until Africans start building structural systems that allow people of all socio-economic classes in society to be able to tap into the many resources on the continent and create wealth, they will continue to depend on the West to spoon-feed them.

Billionaires do not think, plan, and execute on a short term basis. They are always looking and planning ahead. My plan is that before I resign from or retire from my company as its CEO, we will have thought about and written down our 2100 vision. That is what I plan to hand over to my successor. That is how companies that continue to generate wealth from one generation to the next are built. We are building a company that will continue long after we are gone. We are building a company that will keep thriving with its vision untainted from one generation to the next.

These are the kinds of projects that outlive their owners. Examples of such projects include things like establishing schools and building hospitals. I am currently working on some such projects that outlive me. For instance, I envision building schools to raise future leaders. My idea is to integrate educational subjects with teaching on entrepreneurship, where every student will be required to take several classes on entrepreneurship and learn about money. Before graduation, each student should be able to explain what money is and how to make, manage, and multiply it. It will be a mixture of traditional formal education and entrepreneurial skills. The aim is to raise the next generation of billionaires and to write my name in the sand of time.

Richard Branson, the English billionaire, businessman, and Founder of the Virgin Group, has been working on a project for people to vacation on Mars. I learned Elon Musk is also working on the same kind of vision. Right now, such a goal might appear ambitious and unrealistic, but I believe it will happen soon. Of course, no one can say whether Branson or Musk will live to see its actualization. But it doesn't matter. What matters is that fifty years from now or less, Branson or Musk may not be alive, but posterity will remember them for good because of the legacy they have left behind.

We remember the Wright Brothers today for their tenacity in building the first aircraft. We remember Thomas Edison today for trying 10,000 times before he succeeded in creating the first incandescent light bulb. Many people remember John D. Rockefeller's vision to transform Manhattan into one of the great cities in the world. Andrew Carnegie is remembered for leading the expansion of the American steel industry in the nineteenth century. J. P. Morgan is remembered for reorganizing and modernizing the railroad systems in America and subsequently throughout the world. He is also remembered for initiating the banking revolution. Henry Ford is remembered for the

"What you don't know can kill you."

Model T automobile's introduction revolutionized transportation and American industry. These people have written their names in the sand of time by doing something bigger than themselves. Little wonder their names have continued to live long after their demise, and each generation will continue to remember them for their contributions. It 'is not surprising that the Rockefeller Foundation and the Carnegie Foundation have continued to exist. These billionaires multiplied their influence and businesses because they were thinking about posterity and legacy projects. That is why we remember them till this day.

What would you want to be remembered for in the coming generations? Think long term. Think legacy. Think posterity.

3. Business Migration

Many people have been leaving the country without good planning and structures, which has been of great concern to me. There is nothing wrong with people travelling, and everyone, including our leaders, has had to do it at some point. Even scripturally, some whom God used had to leave their home country before God finally used them. So, travelling is not the issue; the issue is when you travel without a plan. We need to tell people how to travel properly and how they need to prepare themselves.

When people travel and have to go into crime out there, it tarnishes the country's image. Many people would have lived a better life in a foreign country if they had known better. Many wouldn't have gone into crime if they knew of other, better opportunities. The kind of people you associate with determines what you know, and knowledge is power. What you don't know can kill you. What you know is what determines the level of success you achieve.

There is so much value in Africa; it continues to be a place with all the opportunities, but we can't stop people from leaving if they want to, but do they leave properly? That's what we are looking at.

We are going to be considering three parts.

a.   The emotional, psychological, and cultural impact of migrating to a new country.

b.   The soft skills you need to have to be able to work professionally abroad

c.   Business opportunities in the diaspora

a.   The emotional, psychological, and cultural impacts of immigration to a new country

A young man interned with us in one of our international offices. I asked him what he was doing in Nigeria, and he said, "My wife and I used to work in the bank." "We were doing very well, but I decided to migrate for a better life." He was in Dubai with his wife and didn't have a job, so he came for the internship in our office. That wasn't looking good, so I asked him if he thought he had made the right decision. He kept saying he still thought so, despite not having a job and the wife being pregnant. Recently, he went to the hospital and learned that the cost of having a baby in Dubai is not something he can afford. He didn't even make that in the last year. So, he reached out to me and said he needed money to send his wife back to Nigeria to give birth.

We must consider many issues before relocating—emotional, psychological, and cultural factors. It's imperative.

The economic system in many of the foreign countries we visit is capitalism. Capitalism is the concept of value for money, which means that you don't deserve anything other than what you earn. It is different in a communal setting such as Africa; you can get things by being related by blood or being friendly and kind.

In America, a father called the cops on his son, claiming he was over 18 and should leave the house. The cops came and threw the boy out. That can't happen in Africa. There's a vast cultural difference and shock that people aren't prepared for when they get out there. So much socialization goes on in the communal system, unlike in the capitalist system. There's always a party to catch every weekend in Africa, where you dance and rejoice. You're not going to have these abroad, which affects you psychologically. You may not even have a chance to say "hi" to your neighbour.

What is the solution?

Build your support structure before you leave. For example, if you're a Muslim, you can look out for a Muslim association to join where you're going. If you're a Christian, you can contact a pastor or church abroad and tell them you're coming. Don't be a burden to them, but keep them in mind if you require assistance. Don't live in isolation; isolation is dangerous to your mental health. Also, look out for professional bodies and cultural associations.

Make sure you contact them before you leave. It's important. In many cases, these structures will help you navigate your career path and get a good job. So, if you do not get in touch with them before you travel, you might run

"Build a solid support system before you travel. It will go a long way toward helping you."

You get into trouble, as you may be too busy or confused to start connecting when you get there.

A woman was asked by her friend to come abroad. She went and started working even without a work permit; she was using the permit of her friend. When the salary came, everything went to her friend's account. The friend divided the salary into two, and when she protested, she claimed the free food and accommodations she had been enjoying.

The person is not evil; that is just the system over there.

Another woman opts for an arranged marriage to travel. She discovered that the supposed husband was using her like a sex machine. So, on the plane, on the journey, she arranged with another man to escape the arranged husband. She got to the new man's place, met his wife and family, and started living with them, only to discover later that, after some time, the new man wanted to sleep with her. She couldn't just elope because all her documents were with the first guy.

So, build a solid support system before you travel. It will go a long way toward helping you.

b. The soft skills to have

We do many things in Nigeria that nobody sees as a big deal. Many of us have not worked on our soft skills to be able to work professionally abroad.

Africa is a communal setting; there is a sense of family responsibility. My money isn't just mine alone but that of my wife, brother, family, etc. When you get to other parts of the world without developing your soft skills, you'll carry the communal mindset there and think everyone is wicked. You can find help on the street in Nigeria. You can go to someone's house unannounced. You can't do that in America, even if you're family; you can't barge into people's homes without telling them beforehand.

"When you get to other parts of the world without developing your soft skills, you'll carry the communal mindset there and think everyone is wicked."

First of all, you have to put together a good curriculum vitae.

Then, it would help if you learned how to put your CV together to suit the country you're considering and take courses on how to pass a job interview in the new country you're going to because the interview method may differ from where you're coming from.

Other soft skills include emotional intelligence. You can watch videos on emotional intelligence. Many other cultures are not as aggressive as we are in Africa. In Africa, we could be aggressive with how we talk, but that doesn't mean we hate you or are wicked. For example, we shout a lot, but this is normal and healthy energy in Africa.

You should learn about emotional intelligence and how people behave or react when angry. You have to read about their laws and a couple of other things.

c. Entrepreneurial or business opportunities in the diaspora

There are specific jobs you can do, even without a degree, that pay over $80,000 a year; for instance, a lady went for her master's degree in the United Kingdom and was doing a part-time job. She then noticed that she could not concentrate on her studies because of the nature of the job she took up. She felt the job was eroding her dignity.

There's nothing wrong with taking up a job, but you shouldn't continue with a job that tends to erode your dignity and self-confidence. That is why, before travelling outside the country, you should be familiar with the businesses you can do there.

"There's nothing wrong with taking up a job, but you shouldn't continue with a job that tends to erode your dignity and self-confidence."

I'll be focusing on the jobs you can go into if you don't have a certificate or your degree is unacceptable. Try and "notarize" all your documents before you travel. That is a process of confirming that your certificates are legit, and it has to be done from the country you are coming from. It gives your certificate a higher chance of being accepted.

If you were a lawyer in Africa who has been called to the bar before moving to the U.K, you could start working as an international lawyer, but many do not know this, and you see them taking menial jobs.

There are specific programs or certifications you can put in for, and before you know it, you'd be earning much better than those with degrees.

Highest Paying Jobs for People Without a Degree

Commercial Pilots: A commercial pilot earns $121,000 a year, and you can become a certified pilot with a license in six months.
Transportation, Storage, and Distribution Manager: You earn about $95,000 a year. You can study these things on Udemy to get your certification as a transportation, storage, and distribution manager. With that, you can start earning a decent income. I'm not saying you shouldn't pursue your degree over there if you want to, but you can start earning a decent income from the first day without having to do a menial job you won't be proud of.
First-line supervisors of police and detectives: These earn about $91,000 a year.
Power plant operators, distributors, and dispatchers earn $85,000 a year.
Elevator and escalator installers and repairers earn $84,000 a year.
Postmasters and mail distributors, petroleum pump system operators, and refinery operators earn around $75,000 annually.
Medical coder: $45,000 a year.
Real estate broker: As a real estate broker, you can earn over $70,000 a year, and it takes just about three months to get

certified.

Margin department supervisor

- · Others are signal and track switch repairers, light technicians, media and communication equipment workers, and air traffic controllers.
- Farmers, ranchers, and other agricultural managers
- Gas plant operators
- Personal trainer: This is one of the world's highest-paying jobs because many wealthy people want their trainer, mainly if you build a brand around it.

You don't need a degree for these jobs; you can easily get certified in less than a year and earn a decent income. You can Google them: "List of high-paying jobs—just certification." No official degree is required for some of these jobs yet, for example, cyber security. You can get a certification in cyber security or as an emergency medical technician and earn a decent yearly income.

I am giving you this because I understand that all fingers are not created equal. I had enough to maintain my businesses even when they were not yielding income. But many of you only have enough to travel, and you would need to pick up some of these part-time jobs to help stabilize yourself and your business

CHAPTER TWELVE

HABIT 11: BUSINESS HABITS

"Change, they say, is the only constant thing in life."

The success of every business rests on certain attitudes, skills, and experiences that combine to form habits. These same factors also determine the failure of a business. billionaires understand certain business principles that bring success. In this section, we examine two specific business habits of billionaires that are a guarantee for success if they are skilfully applied.

1. Multiple Businesses

Change, they say, is the only constant thing in life. One of the characteristics of contemporary societies is the reality of life being in a constant state of flux. Billionaires understand the reality of change and are constantly adjusting themselves and their businesses to meet contemporary trends and demands. Not only do billionaires study and adapt to change, but they are also not afraid to try new things. Billionaires are never afraid to try new things, but they do so with caution and carefulness.

One of the ways to become a billionaire is to be adventurous enough to try new things. People who are not afraid to try new things often discover certain gifts and capabilities that they had not previously thought they had, and with such realizations, often come to a business idea that expands and multiplies their financial status. In short, billionaires own multiple businesses. That is one of their secrets to success. To build wealth, you must be willing to try new things, even going into unknown territory. But you don't go into unknown territory unadvisedly. Never be afraid to try new things because you may never know what specific idea could become your business breakthrough.

"To build wealth, you must be willing to try new things, even if it means going into unknown territory."

While most billionaires own multiple businesses, they are often known for only one thing. In the following discussion, I will explain the principle that billionaires use to own multiple businesses and succeed at them. They don't begin their entrepreneurial journey by dabbling in several things.

Billionaires frequently focus on one business and turn it into a brand before diversifying into another venture. At the same time, they never limit themselves to one thing. They are always thinking about expansion. Therefore, they often end up owning multiple businesses. But while they may own multiple businesses, most billionaires usually choose to focus on one.

Here is a practical example. Bill Gates is popularly known as the Founder of Microsoft, but not many people know that he owns more than 100 businesses. But how does he manage to succeed at this? His secret is simple: He did not try to start multiple businesses all at the same time. Instead, gates spent at least two decades building Microsoft to become a world brand before he considered owning other businesses.

That is where many poor people get it mixed up. They think of the concept of multiple businesses as a fancy catchphrase and do not understand how people who become successful business owners play the game. So, they jump into starting multiple businesses simultaneously and later discover that they have become scaled businesses—jacks of all trades, masters of none.

Billionaires always focus on one business, which grows to become their breakthrough business. And that game-changing venture becomes their signature venture, with which everyone associates them. However, they often invest in multiple other businesses. It is only after becoming a brand and

"Never trade quantity for quality."

building a certain level of wealth that Billionaires diversify and start other businesses.

That is a key principle to always keep in mind when owning multiple businesses. Never trade quantity for quality. By this, I mean do not be tempted to start multiple businesses simultaneously and expect them to be productive. If you are considering starting multiple businesses, you must concentrate your energy, time, and resources on something that you do well and grow it to a strong financial foundation before considering diversifying. Remember, where energy goes, energy flows. What you give the most attention to multiplies. But if you divide your attention too soon among different businesses, you may end up with multiple good business ideas, but none of them may succeed.

For example, when Jeff Bezos—the richest person in the world at the point of writing this book—resigned as the CEO of Amazon in 2020, he was asked what he would be doing after his resignation. He said he wanted to focus on the other smaller businesses he owned. Can you see how billionaires think? So, the Founder and CEO of a multi-billion dollar company resigns from his position to focus on other small businesses that he owns that are not currently well known.

When a poor man starts a potable water business today, instead of concentrating all his efforts on building it up until it becomes his breakthrough company, he wants to run a car business and other businesses simultaneously. That is why many poor people who start a business fail. They often lack the patience to concentrate on one thing, specialize in it, and become known for it before moving on to other things. In the end, they all burn because they have many hot irons in the fire.

Because most poor people who start businesses lack this basic understanding of the operational principles of having a specialized and branded business before diversifying into other areas, they are always frustrated and ineffective since they put their hands in too many things without succeeding in any of them. That may explain why such people always receive multiple phone calls about different things that confuse them and are inefficient. In fact, because of their inability to focus on one thing, most of these people are at risk of developing high blood pressure.

The other day, I was talking with a friend, a partner in our company. He needed something at one of our properties for which he is a contractor. He approached me directly about it. I redirected him to the appropriate people in our Gtext company—the accountants and other operations managers handling such cases. At first, he seemed bewildered that I had to direct him somewhere while I could help him directly as a friend. I had to make him understand that this is not how I operate my businesses. If I decide that I want to know and monitor all the money that comes into the companies that I manage, I will drop dead because I can't keep up. But that is typically what poor people do. Poor people want to engage themselves in too many things simultaneously, resulting in confusion and inefficiency. They are always chasing shadows because they want to oversee everything at the expense of their mental and psychological well-being. That is why they often end up unproductive and frustrated because of the divergent demands of the many unsuccessful things that they seem to be chasing all at once.

When it comes to employment, a poor man may have a good-paying full-time job, but instead of concentrating on that job and giving it his best while saving

"...engage in multiple businesses, but focus only on one thing at a time."

He may be tempted to get involved in other separate businesses along the way. Because he is not focusing on his job and giving it his best, he might get fired because of his inefficiency. And what becomes of his other businesses? They all collapse because he does not have the emotional courage and financial capital to sustain them. He has become a hapless person who lost a fortune because of impatience and too many unnecessary distractions. Such are the kinds of mistakes that poor people often make because of a misunderstanding of the concept of having multiple streams of income through business. Aliko Dangote, for instance, is the owner of multiple businesses. But Dangote does not run all his businesses. He is smart enough to know that doing so will considerably distract him. So, he concentrates on one aspect of his business at a time while he appoints many CEOs and managers to handle his other businesses. Right now, it seems his primary focus is on the refinery he is building. That is where his attention is entirely concentrated. Does it mean he neglects his other businesses like Dangote Cement and Dangote Flour? Certainly not! He knows about their operations, but he has put so many capable hands in those areas that he does not have to worry about what is going on there. This is a crucial principle about the billionaire mindset: engage in multiple businesses, but focus only on one thing at a time.

Most poor people only have one source of income, but they try to do many things simultaneously. In the end, everything suffers. One business principle that I have always taught the people I coach is that if you are an employee—if you have a good job—then focus on your job and make sure that you save enough from your salary and find a way to set up a business that does not require that you run it. That is how to keep your current job and still have another source of income coming into your bank account. But if you try to concentrate on different things demanding your attention, you may lose them all. So never chase multiple things simultaneously without having a stable one.

To avoid the temptation of starting multiple businesses prematurely, you must carve out a niche for yourself and work hard to become known for it. Doing so opens you up to the world and establishes your credibility. When the world recognizes you as someone who has done something credible, it is much easier for people to trust you when you venture out into other niches. The reason is that they know that you have done something incredible before, and they have little or no doubt that you can do it again. But if you rush into too many businesses too soon without being known for anything, people will likely perceive you as someone who lacks focus or is too ambitious.

Choosing a niche does not necessarily mean building companies like Microsoft, Amazon, Apple, or Google. Instead, it means whatever you set out to do, give it your absolute best and work hard to be known as someone who does it better than others. That is the credibility test that makes billionaires succeed.

For it to become a brand, in 2006, Bill Gates became one of the primary owners of Four Seasons Hotels and Resorts, owning nearly fifty percent of the company's equity. That is just one of many such businesses that Bill Gates owns. But many people around the world know him as the founder of Microsoft. Even though Gates' name has become almost synonymous with Microsoft, he has refused to confine himself to the company despite its enormous success. So what is his secret for success in other business ventures unrelated to his technology company? The answer is obvious: It is because he has created a niche for himself that speaks for him anywhere he goes.

Billionaires always have a specific niche they are known for, but that does not stop them from trying other businesses in unrelated niches. That is why they

"When you have a niche, you must work hard to become a brand."

may be known as the founders of a technology company but still, have the leverage to own hotels or food businesses. A billionaire may carve a niche for himself in real estate, but he may also own aviation, sports, E-Commerce, and technology businesses.

The point I have been trying to make is that those billionaires embrace having multiple businesses because they see it as a way of expanding and growing. So they are never afraid to try something new. But they only do so after a massive breakthrough in a specific niche.

You must be determined to work hard to become a brand when you have a niche. The world of business operates on the principle of branding. A brand, by definition, is a specific signature by which a business is known. It always has an identifying symbol, sign, mark, logo, name, word, mantra, or mode of operation. For instance, companies like McDonald's, Nike, Starbucks, Google, Apple, and Facebook are world brands. Brands are often used to distinguish one product from another. But there are also national, regional, geographical, state, ethnic, and local brands that can be involved in every kind of venture. You can have clothing, music, church, comedy skit, talk show, writing brand, and anything imaginable.

Billionaires rely on our perseverance and determination to build the brand. That is because many people who want to start a business often lack the patience and resilience to stick with it long enough to make it a brand. Instead, they start a business today, and after a couple of months, if the results don't seem to be what they had envisioned, they abandon it and start another one. At other times, they rush into starting multiple businesses without specializing in any.

"The world of business thrives on brands."

The world of business thrives on brands. Therefore, every billionaire is a brand. When your business grows to become a brand, people can develop a sense of cultic loyalty to what you offer them. Have you ever wondered why some people are so attached to specific computer, phone, car, clothing, shoe, watch, church, and music brands? The reason is that they have become so accustomed to certain brands that they are willing to pay anything to have that brand. That is how brand loyalty—customers' positive loyalty to specific brands—is used in business. You have a stable business if you are lucky enough to grow your business to brand loyalty status. At that point, considering other business ventures will not cause any harm to your breakthrough business.

As such, when billionaires become brands, they do not limit themselves to one thing. Instead, they begin to have invested interests in multiple businesses. But they do not do so at the detriment of other businesses they own. Take Elon Musk, for instance. He entered the business world by co-founding PayPal, an electronic payment system company. But today, he is the CEO of Tesla and SpaceX. Musk and his partner sold PayPal for about two billion dollars, and Musk used his part of the money to start Tesla and later SpaceX. And most recently, he has invested a lot in bitcoin.

Billionaires own multiple businesses. However, they focus on one business and make sure it has grown before they use it as a base for going into other businesses. As a result, they may be associated with their breakthrough businesses, but not many people know they are shareholders in many other businesses.

"The art of scaling means having the ability to grow without being hindered."

Poor people who try to start multiple businesses often miss this point. Because they learn that billionaires own multiple businesses, they try to dabble in too many things at once without specializing in any or getting a breakthrough. The result is regret, envy, resentment, and bitterness that their efforts are not bearing fruit. They fail to realize that they have become jacks of all trades and masters of none.

Before deciding whether you want to run multiple businesses, you must remember that owning a business is different from running a business. Rich people may own multiple businesses but always run one at a time. Owning a business means hiring staff to execute the daily operations of businesses without being unnecessarily agitated or concerned about what is going on in the company. But running a business means playing the leading role in providing specific directions about the business's daily operations. Most of the multiple companies that billionaires own have nothing to do with their daily operations because they have put a system of checks and balances in place that makes such businesses succeed without their constant monitoring and supervision.

2. Scaled business

Knowing when to scale a business is as important as the business itself. Scaling a business means having the ability to set the stage to enable and enhance support and growth for your business. It means expanding the business and taking it to the next level. The art of scaling means having the ability to grow without being hindered. It means injecting money into your business and revenue engines while ensuring that you have the right people in the right places. But scaling is more than a mere growth in numbers. It means the ability to apply certain principles that will automate and generate substantial revenue

"Every successful business has a tipping point."

for the business. It is not about the size of your business but about the principles of expansion and sustainability.

To scale your business, you will need the support of investors who will be willing to put vast amounts of money into it. As such, scaling requires good planning, organizing, strategizing, funding, and putting the right legal and operational systems in place for effectiveness. It also requires excellent and exceptional commitment and focus. That often requires doing something exceptionally well that puts your business ahead of the competition.

The two crucial things about scaling are understanding the law of timing and mastering the art of using other people's time and money.

Every successful business has a tipping point. That is always the perfect time to scale a business. The Tipping Point, according to Malcolm Gladwell, in a book of the same title, "is that magic moment when an idea, trend, or social behaviour crosses a threshold, tips, and spreads like wildfire." But, of course, we can add "business" to this definition. From a business perspective, a tipping point is where a great idea, nurtured by a great businessman or businesswoman, utilizes excellent human and material resources to scale a business.

Billionaires have mastered the art of scaling. They also know when to take their business public and grow it massively. Since scaling requires knowing the right strategy, people, and timing, billionaires do not take it lightly. They can sacrifice a lot of their comfort to ensure that they grow a business to the point that it will scale without any impediments.

Scaling can be the most exciting period of a business when approached skillfully and timely. But if proper mechanics are not implemented, scaling can be disastrous. That is why it is essential to master the art of scaling.

For maximum scaling of their businesses, billionaires know and understand how to use Other People's Time (OPT). That is, they employ the services of other people who play important roles in enhancing the growth of their business and growing it exponentially. The effective use of OPT is a strategy that anyone who wants to build a business that will grow massively and generate enormous wealth must embrace.

The fact is that no matter how talented, gifted, educated, hard-working, and industrious you are, there is only so much you can achieve. "Two are better than one," one of the ancient philosophers put it in the Holy Scripture, "because they have a good reward for their labour." For if one falls, the other will help him up; but woe to him who falls alone, for he has no one to help him. "And if one prevails against him, two shall withstand him; and a threefold cord is not quickly broken" **(Eccl. 4:9–12).**

Billionaires understand the wisdom of employing other people's services to achieve their business goals and objectives. Using OPT, they ensure that their businesses can run without them. They understand that with the right people in place, it is much easier to scale and grow a business than do everything all alone. A Hausa (one of Nigeria's languages) adage says, *"Sarkin Yawa yafi sarkin karfi."* It means, "A multitude of armies is to be preferred over the military prowess of one warrior." Billionaires know that no matter how skilled and talented they may be, they cannot achieve so much alone. So, they use OPT as an essential strategy for continuous expansion and scaling of their businesses.

"You know you are on your path to creating great wealth when you begin to employ experts and skilled people who understand the business's principles and can work independently in your absence."

On the other hand, poor people are the only ones who carry out all aspects of their businesses. They have not found a way to automate. But billionaires always find a way to automate. That is why they keep getting rich. You know you are on your path to creating great wealth when you begin to employ experts and skilled people who understand the business's principles and can work independently in your absence.

Because I have employed skilled and capable people to handle the various operations of my companies, sometimes I travel to our offices in Dubai, the United States, or the United Kingdom and stay outside Nigeria for three months or more while my businesses in Nigeria continue to run smoothly and thrive. The same thing applies when I leave those countries where we have businesses. Many people in those offices handle the daily operations of my businesses in our various offices outside Nigeria, so even if I decide to stay in Nigeria for several months without visiting those offices, I can sleep well because I trust my employees and partners. As I write this, I have spent my last three months outside Nigeria, but my staff have opened and launched new estates in Nigeria. How did they manage to do that without my presence? Because I have trained them to be acquainted with the company's various operations of the company that I don't always have to be there before something extraordinary takes place. So, while I am busy expanding our businesses in Dubai and elsewhere, my staff in Nigeria are busy opening and launching several estates in my absence. This is what the art of scaling looks like.

To build a lasting business that will scale, you must be willing to put structures in place and employ other people's time so the business can run smoothly and thrive without your constant involvement and monitoring. Because of the lack of such structures, most poor people who start businesses get easily upset and frustrated and assume they are not lucky. Some who work for others may feel that their bosses are giving them too much work and may decide to quit, as advocated in this book abruptly. Unsurprisingly, they quickly discover that their business is not making headway, and they become frustrated and despondent. That is why you keep hearing that more than 90 per cent of startups always fail. One of the primary reasons is that most people who start such businesses often start them out of frustration with their current employers or their socio-economic condition without taking time to put specific structures in place that will make their business most likely to thrive. If you want to save yourself the headache of starting a business that will likely fail, you must be ready, from day one, to use other people's time.

Even when such people use other people's time but fail to put a structure in place that will make their business thrive in their absence, they are bound to encounter massive failure. Therefore, to effectively make use of OPT, you do not only need to employ the services of others; you also need to put suitable structures in place that will make the people that work for you learn to work independently and only report to you occasionally.

What often happens with people who quit their jobs to start their own businesses is that they end up overworking themselves and going through a lot of stress because they don't understand certain basic business principles. For example, some may notice that, after some time, their health begins to deteriorate because of a lack of good sleep and constant anxiety. They started their business under the illusion that it would be a roller coaster ride. Little did they know that such ventures required having good mental and emotional stamina and, most importantly, learning the skills of using other people's time for good productivity.

I always advise the people I coach and mentor that even if you want to start your own business, it would be wise to try to become your boss's best friend so you can learn how he got there. You want to know how successful business people think and the principles and structures they apply in their businesses so you can do it right.

Suffice it to say that employing other people's services is not synonymous with placing the right people in the right place under the right conditions. You may go ahead and employ people to work for you, but if you do not understand the primary ways of using people's skills, talents, and specialities for maximum productivity, you may soon be disappointed. If you hire the wrong people and place them in the wrong places, they may wreak havoc on your business and cause it to fail. You must learn to employ the services of reliable, trusted, proven, and skilled people who will complement your weaknesses and can use their initiatives to work independently to cause speedy growth in your business. Never employ people who will constantly come back to you asking for direction about every tiny detail of running the business. Such employees will end up becoming a liability to you.

Billionaires make sure they put a structure in place that can run without their presence or directions. They always make sure they set up an operational system in their businesses that can run even if they are not there. That, however, should not be mistaken to mean that Billionaires are indolent people who are constantly wasting time away and enjoying themselves while others are working for them. It's not like "monkey work, bamboo chop," as Nigerians say. That idiom translates as "A monkey works while a bamboo enjoys the benefits." It is often used to refer to a situation where

"Smart work entails the art of organizing, planning, strategizing, prioritizing, and skillfully executing a task to achieve specific goals."

one person works hard while another enjoys the benefits without working. That is not what we are referring to here.

Billionaires work harder than most poor people. But most importantly, they work more intelligently than the average business person. The difference between hard work and intelligent work is subtle. Hard work entails spending long hours at work to complete certain tasks and achieve desired results. But the person who works hard may not necessarily see his hard work translate into concrete results. Most poor people work hard all year round but perpetually remain poor. That is where the idea of intelligent work comes in. Brilliant work entails organizing, planning, strategizing, prioritizing, and skillfully executing a task to achieve specific goals.

"While many people worldwide (including the poor) work hard, what distinguishes Billionaires is that they know how to work not only hard but also smart."

If you work closely with most billionaires, you will know that most of them work hard. But while many people worldwide (including the poor) work hard, what distinguishes billionaires is that they know how to work hard and smart. billionaires prioritize brilliant work over hard work. Other people may mistakenly see them as lazy people who like to sit idle and do nothing other than watch people work for them, but billionaires work more with their minds than with their physical strength.

When it comes to their job, billionaires understand that being a business owner means their business can run without them. But poor people do what could be referred to as "self-employment." Self-employment is a situation whereby the owner of a business is the one who is responsible for running every aspect of the business. A poor person thinks he is maximizing and utilizing his resources when he does everything himself. He is ignorant that doing so limits his chances of expansion and stunts his growth. While there is nothing wrong with self-employment, referring to it as "owning a business" is a misnomer. Self-employment is a poor approach to business because nothing can work without the owner's presence and active engagement. The day the owner dies or encounters a severe physical, psychological, or spiritual challenge that incapacitates him, that is the day the business crumbles. Everyone cannot help but watch what he has worked hard to build crumble without help.

As you think about starting your own business, you need to realize that there is a difference between a product and a business. Having the right product alone is not sufficient to make your business succeed. You must have the right product and understand the principles of business operations. Businesses often fail not because the product is wrong but because the owners do not know how to operate the business. A good product in the hands of someone who does not understand business principles is as good as a failed business.

A product is a service(s) you plan to bring to the marketplace, while a business is how you successfully make that happen. Having a product, therefore, does not qualify as having a business. Many poor people have a good product, not a business. You must understand that investors do not invest in products but in businesses. The litmus test to ascertain whether you have a business is to ask if you can leave your business for six months and nothing will go wrong because you have put suitable operational structures in place that work well in your absence. That is when we know that you have a business.

"The fact is that no one can scale a business without using other people's money."

Besides using other people's time (OPT), billionaires also know how to use other people's money (OPM). But billionaires only scale their businesses with OPM after gaining social capital. Many poor people lose sight of it here. Many poor people start raising money for their businesses even before starting them. They think that by trying to raise money for a business they have not started, they will have an advantage in scaling quickly. But billionaires don't do that. They make sure they start a business and grow it to a certain level before scaling. It is only after gaining social capital that they start asking for OPM.

You can see this pattern with billionaires owning Tesla, Uber, Amazon, Microsoft, and many other companies. The owners of such companies only started using OPM in large quantities after they had gained social capital. People knew what the business was and understood the concept of the business. That way, many of the people who bought shares with them already understood the *modus operandi* of the business. Before Aliko Dangote, Africa's richest man went public with his company, investors understood his business model and were willing to put their money into it because the business had proven to be working.

When you start your business, you want to use whatever you have to test-run it and grow it to a certain point before asking people to invest in it. As a rule, you should only scale your business after running it for some time and achieving success. That way, when you announce your intention to go public, investors will not hesitate to put their money into it because they understand that you have a business and your principles have proven to work. In other words, you only scale your business after you have demonstrated the value of the business. The fact is that no one can scale a business without using other people's money.

Billionaires have studied and mastered the art of scaling so much that when they do, people rush in to put their money there because they are confident that they are putting their money in something that has been demonstrated to be worthwhile over time. That way, even if such businesses eventually fail to yield the profit they projected, investors do not become unnecessarily hard on themselves for being unwise, nor do they blame the business owners for playing a ploy on them. They would think that maybe something went wrong, and that was why the business model failed. That is what they will try to find out. They will not try to take the business owner to court unless there is clear evidence of recklessness and mismanagement of resources.

But for many poor people, the moment they have a business idea, they want to ask other people to give them a loan or invest in their idea. While there are confident investors, like angel investors, that may want to take a chance on such initiatives, the majority of investors only invest in businesses that have proven over time to be workable and to have a standard operational principle. If you make the mistake of collecting people's money before starting your business and you are unlucky, and the business fails, you ruin your reputation, and many will find it difficult to trust you in the future, even if you bring up something legitimate. People may call you names, and some may even take legal action against you by labelling you a thief, scammer, or the like. Remember, investors, care about track records.

Earlier, I decided that I would not start raising capital for my real estate company until after we had successfully run the business for some time and built a name and credibility for ourselves. Having demonstrated credibility and shown the world that we know what we are doing, we can scale and ask others to invest in our company. I can confidently say that we have already achieved that status. We have demonstrated how to acquire land in the correct location. Since we have already built a structure and a brand and have become a multi-billion naira real estate company in Africa, if we decide to scale today and ask people to invest in our company, do you think anyone will be suspicious of our operations or doubt our credibility?

CHAPTER THIRTEEN

CONCLUSION

"The best time to have planted a tree was twenty years ago; the second best time is now!" (An African proverb.)

The above quote will serve as a means of summarizing all that this book aims to deliver to the reading audience. The best time to have begun this journey to becoming a billionaire would have been when one was younger with fewer encumbrances. However, now is the second-best time to work towards financial gain and freedom.

Employees of companies should begin to study their employers and the structures and systems in their target industry. Then work assiduously to keep funds aside to further your business interests.

To existing business owners, it is never too late to reassess your business structures and see how you can begin to work hard and smart. Use the principles outlined in this book to get started on your journey to financial emancipation.

With this book, I hope that I have been able to expand the frontiers of your mind, to the extent that you can see that becoming a billionaire (or being wealthy) is attainable in this lifetime.

See you at the top!

Dr. Stephen Akintayo

He is Africa's most influential Investment Coach. He is a member of the Forbes Business Council, an invitation-only organization for successful entrepreneurs and business leaders worldwide.

He is a Serial Entrepreneur and the GMD/CEO of Gtext Holdings, the mother company of different subsidiaries, including Gtext Homes, a Real Estate company with a highly innovative and young workforce, owning over 20 estates. It is based in Dubai, with Headquarters in Dubai, UAE and other branches including Omole Phase 1, Lagos; Abuja, FCT; Ibadan, Oyo State; Abeokuta, Ogun State; Asaba, Delta state, and Port Harcourt, Rivers State, all in Nigeria. Gtext Homes also has offices in London, United Kingdom and a proposed office in Dallas, USA. She has a workforce of over 300 people.

Other subsidiaries include Stephen Akintayo Consulting (SAC), having its Headquarters in Dubai, UAE. It is poised to raise entrepreneurs who will lead the world of business and investments in Nigeria, Africa, and the world. It raises these entrepreneurs through mentorship, practical and in-depth training in courses such as; Real Estate brokerage and investment, E-commerce, Digital marketing, Cryptocurrency, Forex Trading, Stocks and Shares, Business Structure and Grants, Talent Monetization etc. Stephen Akintayo Consulting has a vision of raising 1 million millionaires by the year 2050, with 70% of them from African heritage and others who are Africans in the Diaspora which led to the creation of Stephen Akintayo Online Wealth University in 2020.

The Stephen Akintayo Wealth University is an Online Wealth Creation School. Dr Stephen formed after realizing that formal education doesn't teach about money and wealth creation. Hence, a university that does that was created for people to study and get certified upon completion. This university aims to broaden the knowledge base and further sharpen the skills of young people with our numerous practical and time-tested courses.

Another outstanding subsidiary is Ginido (an E-commerce platform), formerly Gilead Balm. It has hundreds of organizations as its clients, including multinational companies like Heritage Bank, Guarantee Trust Bank, PZ Cussons, MTN, Chivita, DHL, and GNLD, amongst others.

Gtext Holdings has also diversified into the agricultural sector with the subsidiary Gtext Farms. Gtext Farms has a substantial equity investment in Allanisaqriq Limited, which started in 2012. It focuses on cash crop exportation, with a warehouse at Kano, Kogi, Abuja, and over 100 acres of Cashew farm in Oyo State, Nigeria. Gtext Farms plans to grow into Nigeria's largest Cashew crop processor and organic farm by 2035. Subsequently, other subsidiaries like Gtext Land, Gtext Academy, Gtext Hub, Gtext and Associates, Guest, and Gtext Soft have been formed and have also birthed massive results.

The Founder of Gtext Holdings, formerly known as Gilead Balm Group Services, has assisted several businesses in Nigeria to move to desirable levels by aiding them to reach their clients through its enormous nationwide database of actual phone numbers and email addresses. It has hundreds of organizations as its clients, including multinational companies.

He was born in a very impoverished environment in the Gonge area of Maiduguri, Borno State, in the North Eastern part of Nigeria. He had a civil servant mother who raised him and his four other siblings with her meagre salary. His father's contract business had crumbled before he was born. His upbringing informed his passion for philanthropy. In his words, " Hunger was my biggest challenge. I had to scavenge all through primary school to eat lunch, as I didn't go to school with lunch packs. We were too poor to afford that, but things got better in my secondary school days. Although, my mum would go to her colleagues to borrow money to send me to school each term. Seeing them looking at my mum with utter dismay as someone who keeps begging was humiliating. It hurt dearly. I hated poverty and prayed to help more families come out of it."

Dr. Stephen learned to spell the word "THE" in JSS 1. However, his educational background was faulty. You could easily conclude that Stephen will never amount to anything in life. He spent ages 8-12 in an environment without electricity, within a forest region of Maiduguri-Damboa road. "I laid on a mattress at age 13 for the first time", he said.

At 17, he read his first business book, "Rich Dad, Poor Dad" and the rest is history today. He started a business at the age of 17, selling food supplements by GNLD, introduced to him by his cousin. And his first online-based business was selling E-books he bought for N3,000. He ventured into other companies in the process. However, his main drive to succeed was to compensate a very hardworking mother who denied herself everything to educate her five children.

While a student, he organized students' trade fairs within the students' community. It was during his higher education that his mother died of Ovarian Cancer at the age of 24. That was the most demanding season of his life and business career, as his mother had been his leading financier. If there was anyone who believed in his entrepreneurial skill, it was his mother. One of his staff once said he was not a businessman because of his soft-outspokenness and willingness to share his success secrets with others–qualities he learned from his mother.

"The day you start giving is the day you start living. The day you stop giving is the day you start dying. Give daily to live daily. Give joy, counsel, give smiles, give food and give innovative business ideas, to change the world" - Stephen Akintayo. Dr. Stephen Akintayo's story is true of grass to grace. His only regret is that his hardworking mother died a few years before he got the big break, not witnessing what she had always wished for.

In 2020, Dr. Stephen Akintayo took giant strides that landed the entire conglomerate on the global scene, expanding business networks to 4 continents of the world. As a result, the business empire has grown to a multi-Billion naira corporation, with the vision to take over the centre stage in the Real Estate and Digital Marketing sectors.

He is also the Founder and President of the Stephen Akintayo Foundation, formerly called Infinity Foundation. Infinity Foundation started in 2008 as a student Non- Governmental Organization (NGO) with a group of 13 students who donated N3,000 each to impact an orphanage in Ibadan, Western Nigeria, called Galilee Foundation. The Stephen Akintayo Foundation has aided orphans and vulnerable children and has mentored young minds. The Foundation has assisted over 2,000 orphans and vulnerable children. It has also partnered with over 25 orphanage homes in the country. The Foundation has also cared for victims of Boko Haram attacks in the North-Eastern part of Nigeria. The Stephen Akintayo Foundation focuses on donating relief materials, food and financial grants for school children and entrepreneurs.

It offered grants of 10,000,000 naira to 20 entrepreneurs in 2015, $1,000 for the Instagram business challenge in 2021, and #500,000 naira each to 4 winners of the Billionaire Habits book challenge in 2021.

In January and February 2022, the Foundation gave a total of 10 million naira as a bursary to less privileged students of the nursery, primary, and secondary schools, to aid their learning.

From 2023 - 2027, the Foundation plans to empower over 500 entrepreneurs with a grant of $5,000 each across different sectors, technology and United Nations Sustainable Development Goal (UNSDGs) driven. At the end of the five years, the Stephen Akintayo Foundation would have given $5 million to African entrepreneurs.

He is a prolific author who has 41 books to his name. The best-selling Billionaire Habits book, and the sequel, the Billionaire Codes, have sold thousands of copies globally, with book reviews in over 50 cities, building habits of Billionaires in people. Other books include; Survival Instincts, The Information millionaire, Maximizing your Real Estate Investment, and Managing Family Finance, amongst other life-transforming books.

Dr. Stephen is a media personality in the Television, Radio, and Print media. He ran a series on the radio, tagged: CEO Mentorship with Stephen Akintayo. In 2020, he started the revolutionary business TV Show: Investment Chat in a Rolls Royce with Dr Stephen Akintayo, a perfect blend of luxury, entertainment, and investment talks. The TV show is two-phased, the Nigerian and Dubai series. The Nigerian series has been airing since 2020 on Channels Television and his social media platforms–Facebook and YouTube.

In 2021, he took the show to Dubai and how much of a huge success it was! He also started the Learning Luxury Show in Dubai and is on the 3rd edition of the show. He has also started his podcast called The Billionaire Habits Podcast, which aims to bring successful entrepreneurs on the platform who had a poor beginning and made it legitimately to inspire and educate young people. The first edition was shot and produced in Dubai, UAE.

In February 2022, he started the shooting of his 3rd show, Big Talk with DSA–a political show aimed at resetting the minds of youths and empowering them with the proper knowledge to birth a new nation.

In 2021, he also hosted the Global Property Brokers Conference, the largest Brokers Conference in Africa. It is now renamed to the Global Property Festival with international business moguls such as Grant Cardone, Ryan Serhant, and the number one coach in the world, John C. Maxwell, as co-speakers.

In 2022, he organized the Global Wealth Festival in 3 locations worldwide–Nigeria, London, and the United States of America. The first location of the festival was in Dallas, which took place in July 2022, featuring Grant Cardone as the Keynote speaker.

He also hosted the Global Leadership Conference in Dubai, with Ex-president Olusegun Obasanjo as the Keynote speaker. He has also hosted Robert Kiyosaki, Dr Brian Tracy, and Dr Les Brown on the Billionaire Habits Masterclass webinar–a global webinar organized to instil into young people the habits of successful Billionaires and how they can replicate the same.

He's also the convener of the Believers' Wealth Conference and the Family Finance Conference, which teach the believers of the Gospel of Christ and couples how to build legitimate transgenerational wealth for themselves. He hosts a yearly conference called the Upgrade Summit, held at the beginning of every year to prepare young people worldwide for the coming year and how they can achieve giant strides. His mentorship platform has a broad reach as it caters to personal and corporate development. Dr Stephen strongly believes young Nigerians with a passion for entrepreneurship can cause a business revolution in Nigeria and the world. Little wonder why his business empire is run by young, fly, and rich folks.

His first degree was in Microbiology from Olabisi Onabanjo University, Ogun state, Nigeria. He is a member of the Institute of Strategic Management (ISMN). He also graduated from the Harvard University Executive program, where he studied Essential Management Skills for Emerging Leaders and Real Estate Investment.

In 2020, he was awarded a Doctor of Science, D.Sc (Honoris Causa) in Real Estate Development and Corporate Leadership by the European American University. He is also a trained coach by the Coaching Academy, UK.

He is a multiple award winner, happily married, and blessed with three children; two fabulous boys and a lovely girl.

To invite Stephen Akintayo for a speaking engagement visit: www.stephenakintayo.com/booking or kindly send an email to products@stephenakintayo.com. You can also reach him via +971 58 828 3572 or +2348180000618.

OTHER BOOKS WRITTEN BY THE SAME AUTHOR

1. Billionaire Habits

2. Billionaire Codes

3. Maximizing your real estate investment

4. Start business from ground up

5. How to earn 6 figures from digital marketing

6. Mental wealth

7. Managing family finance

8. Entrepreneurial Tools

9. millionaire freelancer

10. The good, bad and ugly of investing in Africa

11. The story behind the glory

12. Survival instincts

13. Business Mentorship

14. Becoming a sales machine

15. Advanced mini-importation

16. Speaking and writing

17. Billionaire investor

18. Cryptocurrency

19. Information millionaire

20. The online money book

21. Building wealthy relationships

22. Farming is the new oil

23. Visa made easy

24. millionaire blogger

25. Scholarship made easy

26. Mobile millionaire

27. Weight loss

28. Locate

29. The law of poverty and wealth

30. Fastest ways to make money through affiliate marketing

31. How to make fast money from social media marketing

32. Becoming a freelance guru

33. Corporate marketing with email campaigns

34. Digital Marketer

35. Affiliate business cash flow

36. Switch

37. Turn your mess to your message

38. Mobile millionaire 2

39. Becoming a Billionaire land banker

40. Billionaire Habits for Pastors

You can get these books on Amazon or Stephen Akintayo

Store, visit store.stephenakintayo.com, or contact +971 58 828 3572 or +234 818 0000 618, or send a mail to products@stephenakintayo.com.

CONNECT WITH DR STEPHEN AKINTAYO ON
THESE SOCIAL MEDIA PLATFORMS

Twitter - http://www.stephenakintayo.com/twitter

Tiktok - http://www.stephenakintayo.com/tiktok

Facebook - http://www.stephenakintayo.com/facebook

Instagram - http://www.stephenakintayo.com/instagram

YouTube - http://www.stephenakintayo.com/youtube

Linkedin – http://www.stephenakintayo.com/linkedin

Email: stephenakintayo@gmail.com

Printed in Great Britain
by Amazon

43031803R00076